# ONLINE MARKETING
## FOR YOUR
## CRAFT BUSINESS

# ONLINE MARKETING

## FOR YOUR
## CRAFT BUSINESS

HOW TO GET YOUR HANDMADE
PRODUCTS DISCOVERED, SHARED
AND SOLD ON THE INTERNET

HILARY PULLEN

D&C
David and Charles

# CONTENTS

## DEDICATION

To Edie, Patrick and Woody and all the people who love them too #myfamilyarethebest

## Making social networking work for you 38

## Creating a cross-channel content strategy 100

# Foreword

Hilary Pullen and I go back a few years. She has been a guest writer on Handmadeology a number of times, and when she told me she was working on a new marketing book, I was super-excited.

I am a self-taught metal artist and a certified Mig welder. I started designing modern metal furniture in 2004 and I built my first piece in Baltimore, Maryland with my sister-in-law, who is a furniture designer. I found my passion in metal and kept on designing and building, struggling for four years to make a name for myself in local galleries in the Grand Rapids, Michigan area. A friend of mine introduced me to Etsy in February 2007, and it changed my business. I started creating a jewellery line and have not turned back. In November 2007, I had to quit my full-time job because my passion was becoming a dream come true!

I found my true calling when I launched Handmadeology in 2010 and wrote *How to Make Money Using Etsy*. With over 3,000 articles, Handmadeology is a daily blog that talks about how to successfully run a creative business. We have about 5,000 daily readers and a vast social network.

I know what it takes first hand to market your crafts online and Hilary's book is one of the most detailed marketing books out there for creative business owners.

Right off the bat, Hilary is going to teach you the ABCs of marketing: Acquisition - Behaviour - Conversion. I love this! The core of marketing your craft business online is right there. On a daily basis, you should be marketing your craft business and remembering these three principles.

When I first started selling my metal jewellery online, I remember my wife telling me that I needed to start a blog for my business. At first, not even knowing what a blog was, I thought she was crazy. After some persuasion, she convinced me to start one. To this day, it was the number-one best decision I made in my creative business. My blog helped to catapult my jewellery business into the world and allowed me to find my voice on the handmade scene.

From where and how to start a blog to a comprehensive list of blog-post ideas, Hilary's chapter on blogging is going to help you start your blog and take it to the next level. SEO is super-important when it comes to blogging and she has covered that area as well. Be sure to grab a highlighter and get ready to mark up this chapter!

Running an online craft business takes time, a ton of effort and constant learning. If you are looking for a marketing guide to help your craft business thrive, then you need to pick up this book.

Timothy Adam
CEO, Handmadeology

# INTRODUCTION

Your focus is your craft, so you are the very best person there is to promote your craft business. You know the products inside out and have confidence in every stitch, fold and detail. Do you want to make selling your crafts and designs a full-time job, or perhaps create a profitable second income? *Online Marketing For Your Craft Business* will show you how to create an online marketing strategy, to increase sales and build awareness of your craft business.

This book looks in depth at the key principles of content and engagement marketing for your craft business. It carefully explains how to use many of the major social media networks and how to create engaging online content, designed to bring potential customers to your online shops. This book shows you how to set realistic and measurable goals that will have a positive impact on your sales figures and raise awareness of your craft business.

## PATRICIA VAN DER AKKER, THE DESIGN TRUST

Networking online is crucial if you have a small creative business. It is the first step in making connections with people and selling yourself and your work. People often mostly focus on selling themselves via social media, but should focus first on networking and the social aspect of social media. You will need to sow first before you can reap! Start following people (journalists, retailers, trade and craft shows, and role models in particular are a good starting point), answer their questions, retweet their messages and comment or ask questions. That will increase your visibility with them, and then you can contact them often more successfully as they already recognize your name.

In this book you will find lots of practical tips to improve your online networking skills and save you precious time. You will also come to understand how content marketing and online networking can make the difference between a few random tweets and being featured in a publication or blog that could see your brand becoming the next big thing!

You could be asked to design for one of the leading craft magazines or be featured in an article by a blogger, and the next thing you know, you have lifestyle magazines and journalists tweeting you and wanting to feature you and your products. It's all about getting the word out about your products through your online networking and blogging.

In this book I will show you how to market your crafts online in an effective and efficient way using content marketing principles that I have learnt while working in the craft industry. I've also asked a few industry experts for their tips and advice, which are shared throughout the book.

I'll show you how to attract potential customers, how to retain existing customers and how to make social networking more rewarding and less of a chore. Every fan or follower is a potential customer, just as if he or she were a browser who had wandered into a shop on a high street. In this book I will explain how to draw fans and followers into your online shop so that you can give them your warmest online smile and let your passion for the crafts you make and sell shine through.

*Hilary Pullen*

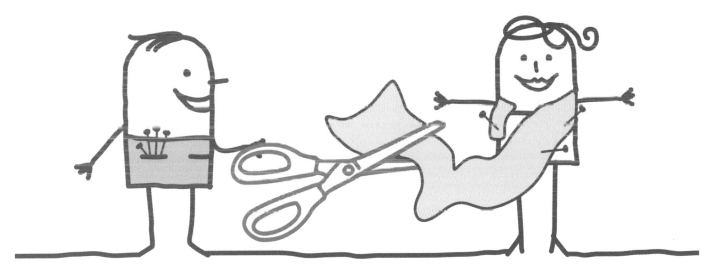

# IS SOCIAL NETWORKING WORTH YOUR TIME AND ENERGY?

## Yes!

The biggest hurdle when selling your handmade work is to get it noticed by people.

With the right content marketing strategy, you can exponentially grow traffic to your site and boost awareness of your brand and your products. If people can't find your work, they can't buy it and they can't tell their friends about it. Social media channels, blogging and networking online can be used to draw people from all around the world to your shop and products.

# The key benefits of social networking

» **Boosting awareness of your work**
Let the right people know your products exist.

» **Brand development**
This is an opportunity to share and develop your unique voice and style.

» **Building relationships with influential people**
Influencers can boost brand awareness exponentially and get you noticed!

» **Engage and inspire an audience of potential customers**
You can use social media to find and engage your target market.

» **Develop loyal fans and brand advocates**
Identify and nurture the important people who will spread the word about your brand.

» **Become known as an authority in your field (an influencer)**
This can open doors and attract influential people to network with.

» **Boosting your site's ranking in search engine results pages**
Social sharing is included in the algorithms of many search engines, and posts can also appear directly in search engine results pages.

» **Creating opportunities for offline networking**
Using social networks can be great as an icebreaker before calling a potential stockist or emailing work to a magazine editor.

» **Market research and product feedback**
You can ask your customers directly for feedback in an informal, chatty atmosphere.

» **Finding juicy content to share**
You can find lots of highly relevant content for blog posts and social media updates.

» **Customer service**
You can quickly and publicly answer your customers' queries.

» **Building confidence in your work**
With every like, comment and share your confidence will grow and have a positive impact on your business.

» **Saving money**
Successful campaigns cost time, but can be entirely free.

# THE ABC OF ONLINE MARKETING

As you read on, I will address exactly how to realize all of the benefits outlined and develop a practical strategy to achieve your goals.

You will begin to see how social networking isn't just about the initial A of 'acquisition' (finding or acquiring people to sell your crafts to) or just the final C of the 'conversion' stage (convincing people to buy). Networking online is also about encouraging specific positive 'behaviour' – clicks and shares of the content you post on social media channels and on your own site.

Your social networking should primarily be about discovering and nurturing relationships with brand influencers and brand advocates – the people who will market and sell your work for you.

The terms acquisition, behaviour and conversion are part of the process of measuring your marketing activity using Google Analytics software. By embedding this terminology in your mind right from the start, you will be able to measure the success of your A B C marketing strategy later on without thinking 'What on earth does "acquisition" have to do with my lovely, friendly craft business?'

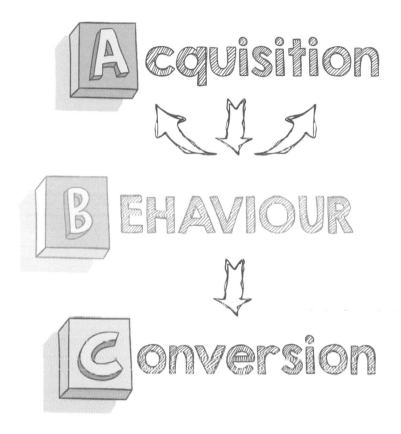

# BRAND ADVOCATES AND BRAND INFLUENCERS

## Brand advocates

Brand advocates (sometimes called brand ambassadors or evangelists) are people who talk positively about your work; they love your products, your service and your style. They share, click and comment on your social media and blog posts. They are your greatest fans and should be your biggest focus.

Your goal is to create a friendly army of brand advocates. Nothing is more effective than word of mouth marketing. If a good friend tells you over a glass of wine or a cup of coffee (or even in a Facebook post or tweet) about a product they love, you will probably take a quick look. Social media channels allow you to create a public platform where your super fans can engage with you – the maker!

### Lara Watson, Mollie Makes

The Mollie Makes team and I find new contributors mostly through online marketplaces like Etsy, in-person at craft fairs and events and, I'd say, most often through social media - particularly Twitter and Instagram. We share with each other the people and brands we're following who inspire us every couple of weeks and always make a note or screengrab when they post images of amazing projects they've been creating.

> Nothing is more effective than word of mouth marketing.

For a fledgling craft business without a huge marketing budget, the aim is to create a free and positive environment to encourage your fans to wax lyrical about your products, interact with like-minded people and generally be positive, interested and excited. See details of each social media channel covered to work out exactly how to do this.

## Brand influencers

Brand influencers are those people who hold sway in your industry – craft and lifestyle bloggers, magazine editors and journalists. This does not mean they have to have a huge network, just a highly engaged network that sits within your target market. They are useful people to get to know. If you reach out to influencers, they may share your message with their brand advocates.

What does 'reaching out' mean? It means having a chat online and making the acquaintance of these influencers. I use the term 'reach' because increasing 'reach' is a term that we use in social media and online marketing to show how many people a post reaches. Influential people can multiply your online reach by shining a virtual spotlight on your work.

# YOUR ONLINE MARKETING STRATEGY

You will need to get this pinned down as soon as possible! Creating a marketing strategy is a way of ensuring that the time you spend online is not wasted time.

## Your strategy needs to show:

» Your craft business's objectives and goals

» Your plans to achieve your goals, detailing action on specific networks

» The time you need to spend on each area

» Your method of measuring success

## Polly Dougdale, Handmade Horizons

Social media is a very important tool, both for engaging your target customer and for connecting with bloggers and publications who might want to feature your products.

Like an online marketing compass, your strategy document becomes a reference for moving forward with your online marketing. It is an effective way of ensuring that you are using your time in an efficient way to develop your brand image and build direct traffic back to your site.

Writing up a strategy really helps to focus your activity and identify your priorities and goals. Don't see it as 'yet another thing to add to the list', but as a starting point that will save you time.

Once you have read through the chapters in this book on blogging, social media and measuring success, you will be all set to complete your strategy document. Make notes as you read – an excuse to buy a new HB pencil and a smart notebook!

## What to include in your online marketing strategy document

These headings are general. I use them when creating online marketing strategies for my clients. As a starting point I find they help you cover all the important basics. A simple Word document is enough; I use an online Google doc and I add hyperlinks to useful reference documents as I go along.

» **Company overview**
Write a really tight description of your craft business, sometimes referred to as your 'Elevator Pitch'. You have to get used to saying what exactly your business is all about succinctly and with confidence. It should be a paragraph or less that quickly sums up exactly what you do. This is not only good for sharing information with an influencer, such as an editor, journalist or blogger, but also great when someone asks you what you do for a living offline.

» **Unique Selling Point: your 'USP'**
Many craft sellers make the mistake of believing their USP is simply that their work is handmade. In reality, you are competing with other artists, designers and craftspeople rather than high street shops. The fact that your products are handmade is fantastic, but it is not a USP, especially if you are selling in a handmade goods marketplace.

Think about the unique design of your products, your choice of certain materials and, importantly, the inspiration behind your design choices. These will all be of interest to your brand advocates and brand influencers.

Write this down in your online marketing strategy:

What makes your work and your craft business better or different from that of competitors selling similar products?

» **The goals of your social media campaign**
Be specific here: what are your goals and do you have timescales to reach them? I have identified the important metrics to measure for each social media channel but these goals should be more about specific conversions and your Return on Investment (ROI) – of time and money. You need to see a growth in income too. You are building your networks, so you need to see more than just growth in fans and followers! The following are Key Performance Indicators (KPIs) for measuring the health and growth of a business:
    There are just three KPIs! Being number one on Google for a search term or having 50,000 visits to your site is lovely, but it means nothing unless you are converting this traffic into sales, sign ups or features each month.

The three KPIs:
* Sales per month
* Newsletter sign ups per month
* Features/mentions per month (links to your website in posts from relevant influencers)

» **Who are you going to target?**
Use this section to clearly define your target market. Again, be specific. If you have multiple audiences, try breaking down your audience into a number of profiles. Really get to know these 'people' and what makes them tick – and click! See the list of questions to ask about your potential customers in 'Identify your target market' in 'The essentials of content marketing'.

What tone should you adopt? Letting your personality flow is, in most cases, the best approach. Consider the audience and identify your style of posts: caring, maternal, witty, edgy or even a little controversial? Will your posts be from you or will you be creating a 'persona'?

For some people, getting into a role can really help set the tone, but you need to be able to maintain this character. It's often better to let the real you shine through so your posts and comments are authentic, believable and sustainable over time.

» **What are the potential challenges of your social media campaign?**
You will need to consider how your social media activity will impact on other aspects of your business. Will you allow or encourage it to be used for customer service queries, for example? How will you deal with negative comments and spam?

*Is social networking worth your time and energy?*

» **Social media networks – specific strategies**
For each network identify your specific strategy, estimate the number of posts you have time to make each day and how you will prioritize your time. Consider how much time you can devote to scheduling posts in advance and the software you will use.

If you have more than one profile to target from researching your market, identify how to divide your time. Is one market potentially worth more than another and therefore deserving more of your attention?

I have created an example of a table of weekly posts (see 'Creating a cross-channel content strategy'). You can use this as a starting point for a weekly posting schedule.

» **Budget**
Make a clear distinction between your online marketing budget and your offline budget, for example, for craft fairs and leaflets. You can specifically measure your online return on investment against your goals and KPIs. Investment could be in giveaway prizes, graphic design services, useful software or advertising. Don't worry if your budget is zero; you can still market your work successfully.

» **Measurement and analysis**
I recommend using Google Analytics and I have outlined the important metrics to measure the success of your social networking, newsletter campaigns and blog content in detail in the last chapter. Monthly analysis is usually sufficient; if you analyse your online marketing any more regularly, you will find you spend more time staring at statistics than engaging with potential customers and influencers. Write down how you will measure success and how often, and the key factors that you will measure.

## ? "How will you deal with negative comments and spam"

» **Keywords**
Create a definitive list here of your target keyword phrases. These are phrases that you want to perform well in search results and to 'own'. You'll discover more about how to use keywords and identify the best to use for your business in the section on blog content.

» **Statistics**
It's useful to keep a record of your blog and social media accounts' monthly growth and link to that in your strategy document. As you progress through the book you will be able to fill in the details and refine your strategy in line with the needs of your own business and the time you have available for networking and content creation. There is no single strategy that suits everyone, but there are some marketing principles you need to master.

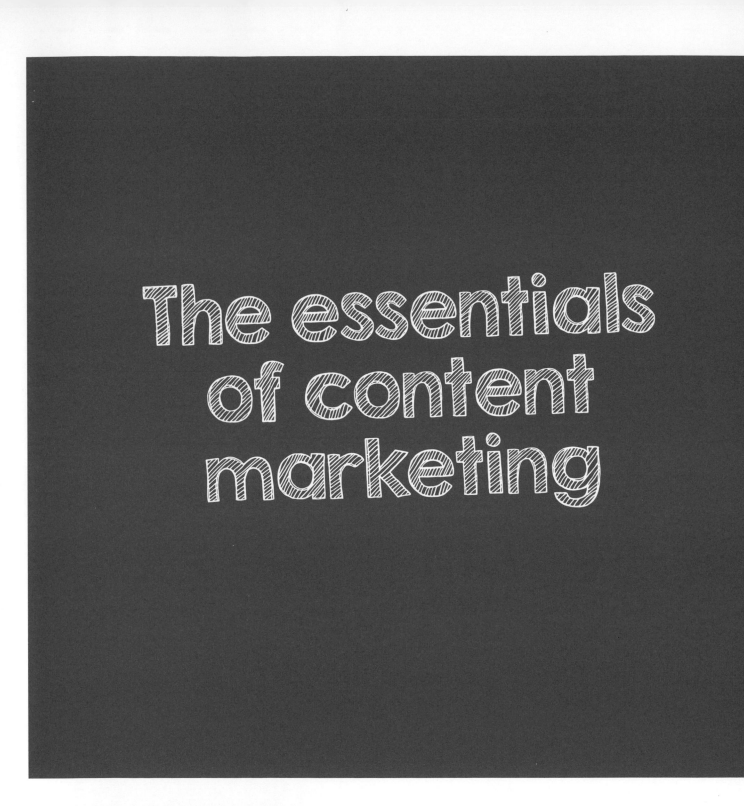

# The essentials of content marketing

Creative people like you are the best at curating and creating great web content. You have an eye for design and beauty and you are passionate about your craft - the perfect ingredients for a successful content marketing strategy!

# WHAT IS CONTENT MARKETING?

Content marketing is a really simple idea. It is the process of driving traffic (clicks) to your site by creating and sharing information, or 'content', designed to interest and engage a clearly defined target market. 'Content' just means text, video or an image. You are enticing your potential customers to exactly where you need them to be – on your site! It is effectively a 'soft sell' because you enable them to find you.

Anything that appears on the Internet is content. The best way to create content is by writing a blog and setting up social media channels to promote your blog posts and connect with your potential customers.

It is essential to understand your target market. If your content is not tailored to a well-defined target market, the people that you bring to your site may not be interested in your products. It quickly becomes a time-wasting exercise – exactly what you want to avoid. Any spare time you have needs to be spent on designing and making your crafts!

## The goals of content marketing

Your amazing online marketing strategy could be bringing thousands of potential customers to your blog every day. . .

But it's all a big waste of time if you don't factor in your conversion strategy, otherwise known as how to get them to (eventually) buy your beautiful handmade goods. A conversion in terms of marketing can be defined as the completion of a goal.

> 'Content' just means text, video or an image.

### Focus your efforts on these goals when creating content:

- » **A purchase**
- » **Signing up to your newsletter**
- » **Sharing your content**
- » **Becoming a fan or follower**
- » **Subscribing to your blog feed**

We'll be looking at how you can measure and improve the success of your strategy using Google Analytics and looking at conversion rates. First, we'll tackle getting the right visitors to your site.

# HOW TO GET YOUR CONTENT DISCOVERED!

There are two ways online content can be discovered. Both are equally important to build up new and returning visitors to your blog or website.

## JAMIE CHALMERS, MR X STITCH

I've been lucky to have found a niche and been in the right place and time to maximize impact on it. There weren't many places featuring contemporary embroidery, let alone the edgier stuff that I do, so I got in there and made the most of it. I've benefited from using social media as outposts for sharing the content from Mr X Stitch, having been with Twitter and Facebook since 2008.

## Referrals

The first way your content can be discovered is through a recommendation from someone; this visitor to your site may have clicked on a Facebook post from a friend or clicked a mention in a blog. Any click that comes from a link is known online as a referral. Referrals from a relevant website need to be celebrated! (See 'Creating a cross-channel content strategy'.)

## Search engines

The other way your online content can be discovered is through search engines, such as Google, Bing or Yahoo to name the three biggest.

### How search engines work

Search engines answer your search queries by checking them against their enormous index of web content. Each search engine has web robots, sometimes known as 'spiders', which crawl the web looking for new and updated content to add to their index.

### Your new job is to feed the spiders!

Don't worry too much about how Bingbots or Googlebots work, it's very complex and they aren't really robots or spiders (thank goodness), just some very sophisticated software applications. But they are very hungry for new content.

I like to remember when I'm thinking about how to get my content noticed that web spiders cannot jump. They don't jump randomly from page to page – they crawl. They can only follow hyperlinks (clickable text or clickable images) on their search for new content to eat up and index.

The higher the quality of the links that come from other sites to your own, the more likely those spiders will visit. I often refer to links being 'juicy' because they are full of Google Juice, which flows from one site to another and also through internal links. If your links are on relevant and influential web pages, the spiders will think your content is important.

When the spider takes a moment to analyse the content it finds on your page, it will say, 'Ah, fantastic! A great new page to add to my list of favourite hangouts'. And the spider is sure to come back. Social networking and blogging create oodles of relevant links for those spiders to crawl happily around on!

### Search algorithms

The search engines look at all the content the spider has discovered and choose which web pages to display in a search query, based on an algorithm or formula. This algorithm is based on several hundred different factors with different levels of importance.

Search engines also tailor search results based on specific users, their location and their search history. This is known as Localization and Personalization. Website owners can no longer say they are number one in Google for a specific term as there are so many factors that now affect which content a search engine will display and there are also lots of ways a user can filter searches. (Search filters are really useful for you to use too – see 'Creating a cross-channel content strategy' for more details.)

Search engines make it their business to know as much about you as possible in order to bring you the best results possible and, of course, to be able to sell advertising.

### KIRSTY ELSON

I like to share other pages/links that I think will appeal to my followers. Not only does it make my Facebook page look more interesting and attractive, but it's also about getting my name out there and making other makers and organizations notice my work!

Just like owning a store loyalty card, your personal Facebook or Google+ profile is a way of letting search engines know your interests and so tailor results and advertising ever more carefully to your tastes. Some people think that Google+ and Facebook are, in fact, just gigantic web spiders that eat up all the updates you share and feed the information back to the search engines to process.

Privacy and giant spider debates aside, the ability to target specific people by offering them tailored content has got to be a good thing for your business.

Effective social networking and following a prescribed content strategy will directly influence how relevant a search engine believes your content is. This is because the search engines are increasingly influenced by the response and online behaviour of real people. They want their organic search results to be the most useful they can possibly be.

In order to gauge if something is useful, they want to see some kind of engagement. It could be a click on a link on a page to look at another post or perhaps a social share of the information discovered. This engagement in your content is the behaviour element of your ABC marketing plan. The more interesting and relevant to the reader, the more chance they will engage and the better your content will rank in the search engine results page.

Engagement is what your strategy should always focus on!

*The essentials of content marketing*

# SEARCH ENGINE OPTIMIZATION

Search Engine Optimization (SEO) is the art of making your blog and social media posts more visible to search engines and pleasing the web spiders. This kind of search traffic is known as 'organic' traffic and it is the most desirable kind of traffic because it's FREE! (Of course, you can also pay a content writer like me to keep those spiders happy.) Remember to always write for the REAL people who you think will LOVE your stuff and not the search spiders!

## Search queries

Search queries are the words someone types into the search engine. You have to work out what those words and phrases will be to improve the chances of your content appearing high up in the search results for specific search queries. That's why it is so important to define your target market before you start writing your content. The words and phrases people type into search engines are called keywords or keyword phrases – see the section on blog content later in this chapter.

There are different areas of basic SEO that you need to address in order to get onto the first page of search engines. Research shows that the majority of people click on the results that come up near the top of the list and do not click through to the second page of results.

> Remember to always write for REAL people you think will LOVE your stuff and not the search spiders!

# Search engines like. . .

» **Original content**
Content is KING! Providing high-quality, information-rich content, especially on your homepage, is vital to create search-engine friendly web pages.

» **Blog design and layout**
The spiders crawling your site need to be able to easily find your site and flow around it. When designing your blog and website, think carefully about navigation. Draw diagrams to show how to get to all the pages on your site and add additional (relevant) links onto pages to help ensure the spiders don't meet any dead ends.

Submitting a sitemap to search engines can also help spiders to find content (see Helpful links and resources).

» **Content frequency**
The web spiders are more likely to come back to see you if you regularly post fresh, original content. Some sites produce masses of content every day. Creating a content strategy and editorial calendar will help you to keep content targeted and of high quality.

» **Relevance**
Becoming an authority on one particular topic by writing about many aspects of it will help all your posts to perform better. The spiders will begin to gain trust in you!

» **Engagement**
Creating a buzz of activity around your site is not just good for getting people interested. The spiders are attracted to popular 'buzzing' pages too and will give your page a boost in the search results. Lots of relevant comments, social shares and approval (such as Facebook likes or Google+s) are needed.

» **Inbound links**
Links on relevant sites that point to your blog can see your search engine rankings rocket! Take time to network and build up these links; they are really important. Remember to prioritize quality over quantity though.

» **Quick-to-load websites**
Spiders don't like to keep people waiting. If your site is slow they will report back and the search engine will favour a site with similar information that loads more quickly. Not everyone uses a really fast connection, so keep image file sizes small and clear off unnecessary clutter that delays how quickly your page loads.
  Even some social sharing buttons can delay load times. I use smart layers from 'Add This' on my sites – it's one piece of code for all my content engagement. It is quick to load and looks good.

# Search engines hate...

» **Copying content**
Search engines detect if you copied and pasted text from elsewhere. Adding a credit makes it ethical but not original. If your blog posts are simply a series of copied chunks of text with a few of your own words as an introduction, your blog posts will not rank highly in the search results.

» **Overuse of keywords**
Don't go crazy and use keywords unnaturally – your content has to make sense. Write for people, not spiders.

» **Links with 'bad' websites**
Keep a check of where you link to and from. Being associated with dodgy or irrelevant websites can do you harm. Make sure you keep any blog post comments clear of spammy links and only accept guest posts from relevant and genuine people, not SEO companies trying to build links back to their clients' websites.
  Don't create lots of the same posts with very similar titles but just written in different ways. They will all end up competing with each other, you will confuse the spiders and all of the pages will rank lower. Choose one post and link lots of quite similar but all relevant content to it order to make sure the spiders realize that this is the key post to bring up in a search.

# IDENTIFY YOUR TARGET MARKET

The more brand advocates busily chatting and engaging on your site, the better. This is why targeting the right market with the right content is so important. It's not all about numbers – 50 engaged and active fans of your brand are far more valuable to you than 500 fans or followers that ignore your posts!

## Keep it niche

The goal of content marketing is to bring people to your blog who fit your target customer profile. If you don't have a customer profile written down in your content and marketing strategy, you are likely to end up with general posts that don't reach out to anyone in particular.
  You also need to know who you want to attract in order to work out which keywords and phrases they are likely to be searching for.

## SARAH CORBETT, CRAFTIVIST COLLECTIVE

People share our craftivism images, projects and services online with their communities, which has led to people all over the world taking part in our projects and events to discuss and act on global issues. We have grown very organically through these social media networks, which has led to media exposure, working with large charities and art institutions, and being seen as the go-to-place to learn how to do effective craftivism.

## DEFINE YOUR CUSTOMER PROFILE

» Man or woman?

» How old are they and what is the age span of your audience?

» Where do they live? Do you ship internationally or should you focus on the UK or even just your own county?

» Income bracket? Do they have spare cash or are they looking for bargains?

» Who do they care about, for example kids or dogs?

» What do they care about? Global warming or their appearance?

» What are their hobbies – activities and sports or arts and crafts?

» What are their occupations – do they work in a 9 to 5 job?

» What are their ambitions and dreams – to live in a hot country or to save the whales?

» Which TV programmes do they enjoy? Newsnight or Loose Women?

» When are they online? After they take the kids to school or during their lunch break?

» What irritates them? Do they 'lol' and 'omg' or are they pedants when it comes to grammar?

» Do they like coffee or tea – or just G&T!

## Building profiles

You should write your blog posts and social media updates with these customer profiles in mind. If necessary, build up a number of profiles. You can give them names and create a story around them. The more real and fixed the idea of your customers is in your head, the better. Then you can visualize them and what they might be doing and thinking about at specific times of the day or week.

These fine details may seem irrelevant but they give you a real understanding of who your customers are and what makes them tick, or more importantly, click! This will help you to relate to your customers through all of your social media interactions and it will help you to find them online.

# WRITING A BLOG

A blog is effectively a website that instead of having static pages has blog posts that are regularly updated. Most websites now have blogs, often with the blog posts featured prominently on the home page.

Many people that are new to blogging can't quite see how a blog can be a valuable tool to help grow their business and fan base. Often, they wrongly assume that the company blog is just a place to share the latest news and press releases about their own products. In fact, it should be the heart of your business and the hub of your social media marketing.

## AMANDA CUSICK, KITSCHYCOO

I think that craft blogging can tend to fall into two categories: aspirational or relatable. Personally, I try to be relatable and show the real person behind the business. When it's so easy to just buy from big businesses, giving a face to a small business connects you to the customer. I think it's a particular challenge to blog when you're also selling - you don't want to come across as too 'spammy', so sharing some of your life, personality, challenges and successes creates a connection with your readers and a shared investment in a community of makers, mothers or other small business owners.

## How a blog will help your craft business

» Allows you to connect with your target market using content marketing
» Builds up your brand identity and personality
» Helps to expand your mailing list
» Allows you to develop your social media networks
» Helps you to connect with influencers
» Shares news of your latest products
» Provides feedback about product development
» Gives you an insight into your market
» Creates a 'buzz' about your company.

## What a blog can do for you personally

» Builds confidence in your own brand or new business
» Develops your copywriting skills
» Focuses your thoughts and ideas
» Improves your skills through feedback
» Allows you to express your creative personality
» Helps you keep up-to-date with industry news through research and sharing
» Allows you to develop friendships with like-minded people
» Develops your IT skills.

Blogs are the enjoyable, dynamic and chatty side to the online face of a business. They set the scene and allow your personality or that of your company to shine through.

In a real bricks and mortar shop or at a craft fair, you have an instant impression of the ethos and kudos of the shop or seller, based on visual clues and your surroundings. You work out fairly quickly if you are likely to be getting your wallet out, stopping to browse and pick up a card or leaflet, or simply walking by. A blog can help you 'set the scene' for an online customer.

> *A blog should be the heart of your business and the hub of your social media marketing.*

## The best place for your blog

If possible, your blog should not be a separate site from where you sell your products but a part of the same site.

Keeping people who have discovered your site on your website for as long as possible and getting them to engage and click sends good signals to the search engine that your content is relevant. This will help boost your website in the rankings and get your products and posts noticed.

Many people start selling their handmade goods from online marketplaces such as Etsy. Starting a blog can also be a great way to send traffic to your online shops, such as Etsy, Folksy or Not On The High Street. You can add links to your online shop from your blog in prominent places, such as the navigation across the top and adverts in the sidebars, to ensure your content marketing drives traffic through to where you are selling your work. Some marketplaces allow you to embed your shop into a static page on a blog. This is a great idea in order to keep your potential customers on your site for longer.

To ensure your marketing is working, make sure that the site you are selling on allows you to see where traffic is coming from. Most online marketplaces allow you to use Google Analytics to track visits and have a simple way to set it up.

## How and where do I start a blog?

There are many 'platforms' that allow you to write a blog. They all provide tools similar to writing a document using a word processor so that you can edit your writing and add images.

You can easily customize the look of your blog using the simple blog platform dashboards, which allow you to design the look and add interesting things to the sidebars, images, links or advertising. Your blog grows with every update, becoming a searchable archive of information.

The platforms listed here are designed to be very user friendly. You can also use them all with a domain name, to remove the 'blogspot' or 'wordpress' part in your blog's title.

If you are intending to invest money, a wordpress.org self-hosted blog is a very flexible option that I would recommend. Wordpress is a content management system. Many e-commerce sites are based on Wordpress, with plug-ins that allow them to list products, create directories and much more. There are thousands of themes available and some are free.

If you are computer savvy, you may be happy to set up your blog yourself. There is a wealth of information available on the Internet for any problems that you come up against. However, many people I have spoken to believe paying for a professional to set up your blog and hosting is well worth the outlay, especially if you are not particularly good with computers. It may be a case of balancing how valuable your time is against the costs of paying someone to start up your blog.

The blogging platform itself is irrelevant without the content, so don't worry too much about this decision! You can always move your blog content at a later date.

### BLOGGING PLATFORMS

I recommend the following platforms:

» **Blogger.com:** owned by Google, easy to use and free
» **Wordpress.com:** free
» **Wordpress.org:** self-hosted, not free

## What to put in the sidebars of a blog

You don't want to be sending people away from your site by providing lots of places for them to disappear off to – unless, of course, it's to a stockist of your products.

The only adverts in your sidebars should be for your own products or your best or most recent blog posts. I see lots of blogs that advertise sites that directly compete for attention with the links to their products. Unless you are making lots of money from advertising, it is a waste of time and space to fill your blog with adverts other than for your own crafts.

> *Every post you write should have a purpose or goal.*

### THE GOALS OF A BLOG POST

» **To attract new, targeted visitors through search engines**
» **To interest and engage with your existing fan base**
» **To encourage sharing and grow your audience**
» **To connect with an organization or 'influencer'**
» **To create interest and 'buzz' about a new product or service**
» **To follow a call to action (for example, to join a mailing list, or click through to buy a product).**

## Set goals

Not goal posts but post goals! The goals of your blog posts can and should vary, but it's important to have an end result in mind so that you are able to measure the success of a post and your blog in general.

Use these goals to help formulate your posts rather than writing just anything for the sake of keeping your blog updated. Updating a blog without having a goal in mind is a waste of your time and often why people end up stopping blogging. They resent the time they spend blogging and networking because they see no positive results from their posts.

Having a goal for every post does not mean it needs to be a complex, extensively researched 'keyword packed' essay each time. In fact, you can vary the time spent on each post across the week or month. A post could be as simple as sharing a single funny image. The goal is to make your existing target audience laugh, love your brand just a little more and show this by sharing the link with their friends.

Alternatively, your post may have a very specific goal. Sometimes I write posts that are entirely aimed at connecting with just one influential person to open an opportunity for networking – a post in response to something shared on their own site, for example. The goal of the post would be a comment and hopefully a share from one of their social networks and the chance to get onto their radar and chat with them on a social network.

## What should I write about?

Good question! In general, try to keep your blog posts focused on a particular topic or theme that is complementary to the products you create and will be of interest to your specific target market. It is best to include different types of posts that will appeal to both existing readers and new readers. Let your personality come through by offering your opinion. You don't want to be known just for curating content, but doing so in a way unique to you!

# BLOG POST IDEAS

Here is a list of ideas to start you thinking about different types of content and themes for writing great blog posts – especially useful if you get 'blogger's block' and for adding variety to your blog post archives.

## Photos: always carry your camera

Staring at a blank page can be utterly uninspiring, but looking at a group of photographs that you have taken recently, whether from a day out, a recent craft project or just about anything else, can fill you with ideas for writing. You could also use images from sites such as Flickr, Pinterest and Tumblr, as long as you add a credit beneath the image. I often use the best images from the Craft Blog UK Flickr group to illustrate and brighten my posts.

### Updates: use old posts for inspiration

Did you write a post a few weeks, months or years ago that could be revisited? Open up your post history/ archives and scroll through. You are sure to find something that you could revisit. It is fascinating for readers to see how time has changed us and our crafts and techniques. Linking back to relevant posts is also good for search engine ranking (see 'The essentials of content marketing').

## TILLY WALNES, TILLY AND THE BUTTONS

My blog is at the heart of my business and fuels everything I do - I'd go so far as to say it's the number-one asset of my business. Writing a blog has allowed me to engage with a wide variety of people, develop a loyal audience, conduct ongoing customer research, catch the attention of the press, demonstrate my expertise with publishers, network with other people working in my field - and to do so with authenticity. Oh, and it's a lot of fun!

## Write posts about other bloggers

Visitors that have come to your blog are likely to be interested in the same bloggers as you. Let them know a little bit about the blogs you enjoy reading. Why do you like these particular blogs and how did you find them? Let the blogger in question know you have mentioned their blog – your readers will be intrigued and the bloggers you are writing about will be flattered by the publicity. Make sure you let them know so that they can help to promote your post, too!

## Top 10 and other lists

Top 10 lists, or lists of any quantity, are really interesting to read. To write them, you are forced to make editorial decisions about what to include to create an informative, concise (or humorous) post. You can invite readers to add to your list by suggesting their own favourite, most useful, prettiest, funniest, best or worst item. The ideas are limitless with this type of post. Whether it's the 'best 5 free granny square tutorials' or 'Top 10 funniest dogs on bicycles', these posts are always popular if aimed correctly at your target market.

# INTERVIEWS: OTHER PEOPLE ARE FASCINATING

Email or message a crafter or blogger who suits your target market and ask politely if they would be interested in answering a few questions about their work. Alternatively, write a post in a relevant forum requesting candidates for your new interview slots. Limit the number of questions so it doesn't become a chore for the interviewee or too much for the reader to take in. Try and ask original questions – nothing too personal but something you feel that the readers of your blog may actually be interested in.

## Spark up a debate

Questions don't have to be reserved for forums or search engines. There are many talented people and experts who are more than willing to engage in discussions. The plus side is that you may get some great comments, and your post becomes a resource on a particular subject. If you don't already have a blog readership or social networks, then post in relevant forums to encourage people to share and comment.

To encourage people to comment, invite them to leave links to their own websites. If you get no response whatsoever, then either edit the post and add links to where you found out the answers to your question or add your own comments with these links. That way, it is still a useful post for readers.

## Shop update: goals and achievements

Shop updates can be extremely interesting and really useful for your online business or your development as a crafter. Revisit old posts in order to show your progress, address shortcomings and plan for the future. It makes for great self promotion as long as you don't dwell on anything too negative. Try not to make it simply an advert for your shop, which can be tedious for regular readers.

### Share your expertise

You may have seen questions that other bloggers have asked which fit your target audience or questions that someone has asked in a forum. Why not answer them on your own blog? Flesh out the post with relevant images and then post the URL link of your blog post on the forum or as a blog comment, saying 'I thought this was such an interesting question I had to write a post about it'. You can incorporate other people's responses too, as long as you link back to the thread clearly in your post. You'll get traffic to your blog and hopefully you will have helped someone out too, which is a great feeling.

## REVIEWS

Reviews of products, websites and books within your target market can make useful posts. By writing a review, you are helping others by giving them your honest opinion. Ask the owner of the site or the author of the book if they would be willing to add a quote on your post that adds credibility to your review. You'll find them on one social network or another, and a quote could be as short and sweet as one tweet!

## Regular posts

Think about a themed post that you can blog about week after week, so your readers can look forward to it. If you read other blogs, you may discover groups of bloggers that choose a day to write a post about something, such as 'Wordless Wednesday' or a post about their Craft Space every Monday. These posts can be good for connecting with other bloggers – you can comment on them and let them know you also write themed posts, bringing bloggers to your own blog. The more bloggers you know the better!

## Guest posts

Inviting relevant people to guest post on your blog is a great way to connect with experts in your field or with 'complementary' bloggers. It can make your blog more interesting to hear other voices and opinions, especially if they are an authority on a subject.

You can also offer to write posts for other blogs in exchange for links back to your shop's website and blog. This is a great way to connect with an existing readership as well as improve your search engine optimization with these 'back links'.

*If you see questions on another blog, why not answer them on yours.*

Try to make a connection with a blogger through social networking before emailing them and offering them a guest post. Successful bloggers get masses of offers of 'free content', usually from dubious sources. Make sure you don't get mixed up with the spammers by creating a genuine connection first so the blogger is expecting your email.

## Pillar posts

Pillar posts contain links to other posts and readers love them. They enable a reader (and a web spider) to find links to all sorts of information on one subject. Many of my most successful posts on my own blogs and for my clients are pillar posts that link to a raft of other posts I've written about a particular topic.

You can also create pillar posts that link to other people's blog content. This kind of post is very shareable.

*Having guest bloggers always helps to build links back to your blog too — invariably the guest blogger will help to promote the post.*

# HOW TO USE KEYWORDS

The way you write your posts has a definite and measurable effect on how a search engine will find and rank your content.

## What are keywords?

As discussed earlier, a search engine uses robots or 'spiders' to crawl the web. The spider can only rely on the information (text, images and links) you have posted to return results; it can't infer any information. It is important that you use the right keywords and phrases in your post and put them in the right places.

The web spider studies the text and images on your page, looking at the frequency and position of certain keywords and keyword phrases. It can then match this to people's search queries and bring up the results in the order it deems most relevant to the words used in their search. The order of keywords can also affect position. Be clear about which keywords you want to rank for and ensure you use the exact combination of words.

Here is an example of a simple sentence under an image of some pretty floral aprons in a blog post. We want the post to be found by people searching for pretty floral aprons**.**

'Don't you love the beautiful colours? I love making these as they are so quick but they look great!'

The word 'apron' is not mentioned, even though to a reader the placement infers what the writer is referring to. The web spider will not see the word. Instead you should write:

'The colours in these **pretty floral aprons** are beautiful. I love making **aprons** like this because they are so quick but they look great.'

The text still reads naturally but you have replaced the pronouns with descriptive keywords, allowing a web spider to read it.

## Where to use keywords and phrases in text

### The title of the post

The title is the biggest indicator of the content within, so it should contain the keywords you are targeting. Aim to write unique and descriptive titles – this is best for search engines and ultimately for your readers.

Most blog platforms allow you to adjust the URL (the blogpost's permalink or unique web address). Ensure that you add the descriptive keywords here as well as in the title on the webpage.

In a post about lovely spring handmade aprons for example, the title could be any number of things but you need to be clear about the keywords you want to target. If the key phrase is 'Pretty Floral Aprons', then these words should be in the title and the URL of the post.

# "Does your post sound natural when you read it back"

### The first paragraph

Make this text descriptive of the content of the post and ensure that your chosen keyword phrase is included here. This is the post opener. As with all good articles, it introduces the subject and will reassure the person reading that they are in the right place as well as encouraging them to keep reading. So make it interesting too – it's not just about the keywords.

### The body of the post

Use your keywords in the body of the post too. Take care to ensure it remains readable and you don't overuse the keywords. You'll know if it feels unnatural just by reading it back to yourself.

This is natural use of a keyword phrase:

'The colours in these **pretty floral aprons** are beautiful. I love making **aprons** like this because they are so quick but they look great.'

In my opinion, this is an unnatural use of the keyword phrase:

'The colours in these pretty floral aprons are beautiful. I love making pretty floral aprons like this because they are so quick but they look great.'

Instead I will find another place further down in the text of my post to add the phrase again. Be creative – asking a question is a great way to use a keyword and could result in the comments you get back containing the keyword.

Here is an example:

'Are these pretty floral aprons old fashioned or retro – what do you think?'

Don't use other website's posts that are performing well as a guide to how many times to include your keyword phrase. They may be ranking highly for that phrase owing to an editorial link from a relevant website rather than for the number of times they have used the keyword in that particular post. Make your own decisions and measure your success – that's the only way you'll know if you are making progress.

### In images

When you upload an image to a blog, name the image using your chosen keywords only if the image is actually of 'pretty floral aprons', for example. If you also include an image of your inspiration, such as a bunch of flowers, do not use the keyword phrase here because this would be seen as 'keyword stuffing'. You should get the option to add a title tag and an alt tag to your image when you upload it. Describe the image properly! The title tag is the little text that pops up when you hover over an image and the alt tag is the text that someone whose browser is not displaying an image sees.

Searching by image is very popular and Google will use these tags, the name of the image and the immediate text surrounding the image to decide if it is displayed in search results. Always take the time to label images correctly.

### Internal links

You can turn text in your blog posts into links. If you are writing about your pretty floral aprons you could link to another post where you wrote about the floral tea towels you made. Using the text 'floral tea towels' as the link may help that page's rankings for that term and may help to get the page crawled by a web spider that has found its way to your apron's post.

As we have discussed, web spiders need to be able to crawl your site so take the opportunity to add links to other useful pages within your site. Remember the web spider can't jump or use a search box, and unless pages contain internal links to crawl around some of your content may not be getting regularly crawled.

### External links

A link can help to pass on 'Google Juice' – effectively counting as a vote for a specific page – but it has to be seen to be relevant or else it will have the opposite effect. If you are writing about Pretty Floral Aprons you might want to link to The Museum of Aprons because you think your reader will find it interesting. This is great. The search engine thinks the link is relevant as it flows onto a page that contains the word 'aprons'. The link juice doesn't pass both ways but your page and the links on it are deemed useful and interesting to the reader and are more likely to appear higher in the search engine results pages for searches on that topic.

Don't include too many external links, unless you are creating a pillar post that you hope will be shared virally through social media. You don't want to encourage people to leave your website unnecessarily but you do want your site to be really useful and interesting, so links out are good.

But beware! Linking from Pretty Floral Aprons to a website selling 'organic manure' (I'm being polite!) is not a particularly good idea. The site's owner might offer you money, thinking that because you have mentioned flowers they could get some of your Google Juice by having a link to their site full of manure. You need to carefully assess how this would look in the eyes of a web spider if it follows a link and ends up on a page that seemingly has nothing to do with the keywords on your site.

You must use a 'nofollow' tag on all paid links from your site, including paid-for image-based ads in your sidebars (Wordpress and Blogger both offer this as an option when adding a link), which tells the spider that you do not want to pass on the 'Google Juice'.

Google has created this rule in order to stop link spamming – people paying sites for links back just to help improve their ranking. Google wants sites to earn those links by having great content that sites want to link to in order to make their own site more useful for their readers.

# TARGETED BLOG POST CAMPAIGN

Here is an example of a content marketing strategy aimed at making me an authority in the eyes of Google on handmade environmentally friendly gifts.

Imagine that I make handbags from environmentally friendly, locally sourced materials, which will appeal to people who care about the environment.

After brainstorming ideas for the type of products my target market may be searching for, I decide that writing posts aimed at women looking for eco-friendly products and gifts would be perfect. I could create a series of posts with ideas for eco gifts or with my reviews of eco products, with my own eco-friendly handbags advertised prominently on my site.

My next step is to work out which keyword phrases these people might be searching for.

## Long tail keywords

Using 'long tail' keyword phrases usually provides the most targeted response – for example, 'handmade eco friendly accessories London'.

Research in e-commerce shows that people searching for a very detailed phrase are likely to have narrowed their search because they are close to purchasing rather than just browsing. This makes these search terms more desirable, because even though there are fewer people per month searching, the chance of a conversion (buying your products) is higher. We call this kind of traffic 'highly qualified'.

This is the same when someone is searching for information. If your post specifically answers their query, they are far more likely to engage with your blog in some desirable way (sign up to newsletter, leave a comment, visit your shop or click 'like' on your Facebook page widget) than someone who has been searching for more general terms.

Start brainstorming to work out what people in your target market are searching for – is it gardening tips, jam recipes or interior design ideas? Take these broad terms and then do your research on some long tail search terms.

# "What are people in your target market searching for"

## Using the Google keyword planner

To work out which keyword phrases people are searching for, you can use the free Google keyword planner. It is designed for people using Adwords, but it is helpful for organic SEO too. You need to sign up for a free Google Adwords account to access the tool.

There are other tools available. Search for Free Keyword Tools – some offer keyword ideas and also tracking of your keywords to help you see where on average your site is ranking for certain keywords. You can also pay for keyword tracking and SEO software but I don't think this is necessary when you are starting out.

It's fairly straightforward to use the keyword planner. Just type in your keyword idea, add in filter details for location, and Google will offer groups of similar phrases and keyword ideas. See https://adwords.google.com/ko/KeywordPlanner/Home

| KEYWORD | AVERAGE MONTHLY SEARCHES WORLDWIDE | MOST POPULAR MONTH - NUMBER OF SEARCHES | COMPETITION |
|---|---|---|---|
| Eco friendly gifts | 1,300 | December 3,600 | High |
| Environmentally friendly gifts | 210 | December 590 | High |
| Eco friendly Christmas gifts | 90 | December 590 | Medium |
| Eco friendly ideas | 390 | April 590 | Low |
| Best eco friendly gifts | 20 | December 90 | Medium |
| Best eco friendly gifts | 420 | April 720 | Low |

## Find a focus

Looking at the keyword planner results, I believe I would be best to focus my eco blog-post series around the term 'How to be Eco Friendly' because there appears to be large volume with low competition. I can give a weekly tip on how to be eco friendly, including content each week on the 'best eco friendly gifts' and lots of 'eco friendly ideas' and tips to make or buy, sourced from craft sellers and bloggers as well as some of my own designs.

Remember that competition also varies depending on the location filter you have used. High competition signifies that lots of advertisers are bidding for the phrase in Google adwords. This does not mean you cannot get to page one of Google organically with a really well worked-out strategy and focused networking. However, it suggests that businesses will also be optimizing organic content and you may struggle to compete with both as a new blogger.

## Check the competition

If you find a keyword term you want to use has high competition, check the search results for the websites that are performing best in organic searches for these terms. Add all the sites on the first page of results to your Twitter lists or blog feeds for future networking. Unless they represent direct competition, it could be that you have something to offer these sites and can perhaps work on a guest post for them, or you could create a post all about them on your site as a way of getting noticed by them. The important thing is to have highly relevant content or products to show these influencers. They need to see quality and relevance before they will share any of your posts with their networks or work with you.

> **Keep track of keywords you are targeting in your strategy document.**

If I type in 'eco friendly gifts' I discover 1,300 people per month across the world are searching for this term. I can use the filters to find out how many searches are from the USA or UK, and I can even look more specifically at details of searches in my area using the advanced filter.

If I mouse over the symbol of a graph in the results, it will show me how the searches are split over the year. Unsurprisingly, the phrase is most popular in the run-up to Christmas.

Google also tells me that the competition for this term is high, suggesting a lot of people want to get their content to the top of this search. So I will carry out some research into associated keywords that may have less competition.

The table shows the keyword terms I discovered and the suggested number of searches per month. Google's keyword planner offers 'Keyword Groups', which is a helpful way of looking at related keywords and keyword phrases. Keep track of keywords you are targeting in your strategy document.

### Use low-competition keywords

From my research, I plan to write 10 posts all aimed at eco friendly gifts for specific types of people and I will review 10 eco friendly products. Posts take time to write, so I plan to write one a week alongside some of my more everyday and less labour-intensive posts.

In each post I will target specific lower competition keyword phrases from my research, ensuring that images are also optimized (See 'Making social networking work for you'.)

Since I am featuring eco friendly handmade goods, I will also contact all the designers or makers I have included via social media to let them know they have been featured and invite them to share the post or add a comment. I will ensure that I don't include anyone that I believe is a direct competitor, for obvious reasons.

I hope that reaching out to these designers will also help my bags get seen by some of their own fans and followers who are in my target market.

On my blog's home page I will ensure that I mention that my own handmade handbags make great **eco friendly gifts for women**. I will also create a link on my home page to pillar posts where people (and web spiders) can find all of the links to my posts on eco-friendly gifts and products.

Through promotion of the posts across social media, networking with complementary businesses to my own and creating a wealth of information around the keywords 'eco friendly gifts', Google will begin to see my website as an authority on handmade eco friendly gifts and eco product reviews.

## ? "What should my blog-post series focus on"

# BLOG POST CHECKLIST

» Research your target market and brainstorm an idea for a post.

» Research keyword phrases to include using the Google Keyword Planner.

» Write a draft post.

» Add beautiful 'pinnable' and relevant images.

» Add a call to action to sign up to your newsletter.

» Edit titles, subtitles and body text to ensure keywords are used and correct links and credits added.

» Ensure images have appropriate title tags and alt text.

» Create a leading image for promotion with an added text prompt to clarify what the post is about.

» Read through again to ensure the post flows naturally and is not keyword stuffed.

» Schedule the post for an optimal time in the future.

» Promote the post across all of your channels as soon as it goes live.

» Contact or tag anyone, especially influencers, mentioned in the post – and future posts too!

» Ensure your post is internally linked to past posts.

» Measure your success with Google Analytics and brainstorm more blog post ideas!

# THE IMPORTANCE OF GREAT PHOTOGRAPHY

It is incredibly difficult for designers and makers to get their products noticed amid the huge amount of competition online. A marketing strategy, no matter how well considered and researched, will fall flat if the images shared are dull or low quality. With the right imagery and marketing strategy, your products will become highly desirable.

Product photography of consistent high quality is vital to give your customers confidence in your work and bring in the sales. You can use your images to convey styles and themes, creating a brand style that will become instantly recognizable to your fans. Simple Photoshop software, Picmonkey, Picasa or Gimp for example, allow you to crop an image, improve exposure and overlay text.

Great photographs and videos also pique the interest of influencers, publishers, journalists and bloggers. These influential people curate collections of work and they are always looking for content to share.

> ## PATRICIA VAN DER AKKER, THE DESIGN TRUST
>
> Stunning images are crucial to show the quality of your work and create your branding. Show off your beautiful colours, the high quality of your materials and skills! Especially if you want to sell online you need to attract very quickly your dream clients (they are browsing so you've only got a couple of seconds at the most!). The only way to do that is through good photography and using appropriate styling.

**Your photos need to leap out at the viewer and bite them!**

It takes time and lots of practise to find your own photographic style and learn how to create beautiful pictures of your work, but it's definitely worth the effort if you are serious about selling online. Never share poor images of your work – it looks unprofessional and devalues your crafts.

I adore great photography and I curate my own collection of excellent examples of craft photography. See 'Craft Photography Tips' on my website www.ukcraftblog.com/2011/10/craft-photography-tips.html for practical advice and links to some excellent online resources, including my own series of photography tutorials.

Do not underestimate the importance of high-quality 'branded' images of your work. Take a look at the section on creating 'pinnable images' in 'Making social networking work for you' for more details on how to make your images work harder to bring targeted traffic to your site.

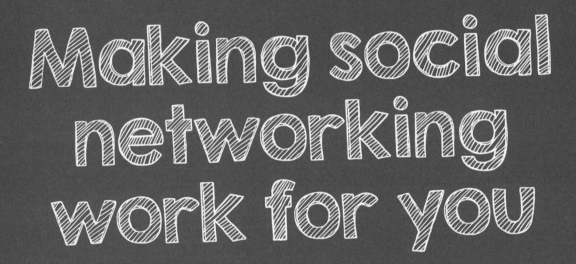

How can you use social networks to find and engage with your target market and connect with brand advocates? While there are many common themes that are true of all social networks, each offers different ways to interact with influencers and build awareness of your brand in meaningful ways.

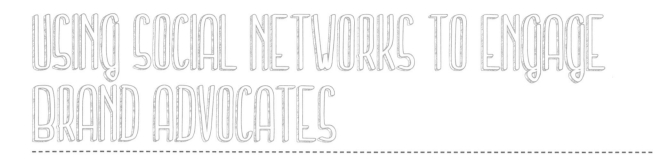

# USING SOCIAL NETWORKS TO ENGAGE BRAND ADVOCATES

You may ask, 'I don't have much time – which social network should I focus on?' The answer is that you need to use them all in different ways for different purposes. The key is knowing the ground rules for each network and understanding how the information you share on that network reaches people.

There is a theory that you shouldn't butter your bread too thinly when it comes to social networking. I feel that with good time management and a focused content strategy you can be active on many networks.

## PERRI LEWIS, MAKE AND DO WITH PERRI

Think creatively when it comes to choosing who to interact with. Big craft bloggers, craft magazines and the journalists who write for them might seem like the best people to follow, but what about interiors journalists, fashion writers or design editors? Find the people who are known for writing about emerging designers and young talent in your area - there are plenty of journalists who have that as their USP and who are always on the hunt for new people to feature.

"I don't have much time - which social network should I focus on"

For example, if I wanted to engage with an influencer who is a prolific Instagram user, then leaving a comment on their latest Instagram picture would be the best way of getting their attention. If I don't have a profile on Instagram I can't do that. It's never just about how many likes and shares. Your social networking activity always needs to be meaningful, and this comes down to your research – in particular, looking at the networks and communities your target market uses.

Content can be shared to many different networks at a time and there are many tools (some free) you can use to save time. I explain the pros and cons of auto sharing and social media clients in 'Creating a cross-channel content strategy'. First of all you need to get to grips with each network in its native form.

In this section, I focus on Facebook, Pinterest, Twitter, Google+, YouTube, Instagram and Linkedin. This by no means covers all of the social media channels out there. But it will give you an insight into the way that you can connect with different types of major social media channels and how you can bring all of the channels you use together for a holistic approach to your online networking.

As you discover channels not covered in this book, and as new networks emerge, you will find they have cherry-picked features from existing networks and you will easily be able to adapt your strategy to fit.

# CREATING POWERFUL PROFILE PAGES

It's time to optimize your profile pages for maximum impact.

The following are practical guidelines for setting up a profile that can be applied to all of your social media networks. The buttons may be in different places but the principles are the same. The profiles you create need to really sing about your creativity, capturing the essence of your brand and the attention of your target audience.

Each profile, while engaging a slightly different social audience, should help to build a recognizable branded feel for your craft business and boost your online visibility. Online visibility simply means that more people can find your business when searching online, internally within a social network or externally using a search engine like Google.

## What is a profile page?

When you sign up to a social network, whether as a business or a personal account, you always create a profile page. This is the page where people can find out more about you and decide whether to follow your updates or contact you.

Social media channels will all ask you to choose a username, write a short description of yourself or your business and upload an image that represents you or your business. Most will allow you to share one or more links to your website or other networks.

It is very simple to open social media accounts. However, it is important to take time to consider the very best way to make your profile both visible in searches and highly appealing to people who visit you. This will help to increase follower and fan numbers.

# Creating a great profile

» **Choosing your unique username**
If you are looking for social media marketing tips, it is very likely that you already have a business name picked out. Where possible, this should be the username for all of the social media business accounts you manage.

» **Research your business name online**
If you are yet to choose a business name, search all the social networks before deciding on a final name. It can be very confusing if your Twitter and Facebook pages have a different name from your business or to each other, and it can make it hard for your customers to find or indeed recognize you if they are already connected to you on a different network.

You don't want a business name that you have to laboriously spell out every time you introduce your new brand – it should be easy to remember and spell. Test this out by calling a friend and saying it over the phone. Did you have to repeat yourself? Did you feel confident saying it and explaining the inspiration for the name? People will want to know why you've chosen it.

> *Be consistent with your username to avoid confusion and help people to find you easily on their favourite networks.*

» **Keywords in your business name**
Adding keywords to your username that identify your industry can be helpful to quickly tell people what you do. For example @Hilaryknits rather than @Hilary. Just be 100 per cent sure that your business is not likely to diversify in the future because not all networks allow you to change your username.

» **Use your own name**
As a designer, using your own name as your business name can make a very clear statement that the products are handmade or designed by you, with your unique style. It immediately personalizes your brand and can make your design label sound more professional.

» **Abbreviating your name**
You may have a business name with too many characters for some networks. For example, Twitter allows a username with a maximum of 15 characters. Take extreme care when abbreviating your business name. Try typing it out and saying it out loud to be sure it sounds OK and slips off the tongue easily.

» **Backgrounds**
Many social networks give you the opportunity to load up a cover or background image. This is a little like the 'hero' image that web designers refer to, the image that immediately captures attention and engages with people who land on your profile page.

This image is an opportunity to add personality to your profile page. These background/cover images can be regularly changed. Take advantage of this and use seasonal images or styled shots of your latest products when you are promoting a launch. Think about how the image is representative of your brand's style – it needs to instantly give a viewer a great impression.

Your avatar should remain consistent across all your networks. but your backgrounds and cover images can vary depending on the network. Just ensure they are in focus and representative of your brand's style.

» **Biographies and keywords**
On all social network profiles, you can write a brief description or biography (bio) all about yourself or your business. This is an opportunity not only to let the visitor to your profile learn more about you but also to ensure your profile contains keywords that fit your brand. Before starting to fill out your descriptions, write down lists of words that people may use if they are looking to connect with a brand like yours. This is really useful for every aspect of your online marketing.

The description or bio needs to read well. Keep it brief and to the point. Not many people will read more than a few sentences and in many cases you will be limited to a certain number of characters. For example, Twitter allows you just 160 characters for your bio. See Twitter networking in 'Making social networking work for you' for some tips on making the most of this limited space.

Being funny and a little abstract can work well because this will encourage people to follow your accounts. Just try to incorporate keywords, too!

## KAREN JINKS, UKHANDMADE

Social media is such an important tool for creatives and independents. Not only does it create an opportunity to engage directly with your audience and increase sales, but it also builds communities. Many of us are solitary creatures, often working alone at home, so having instant access to fellow creatives for support, advice and chat is a lifeline. It's a great way to share and communicate and I'd be lost without it.

» **Links**
It can be tricky to decide which link to add to a profile when you are only given the chance to add one. You want people who see your profile to use this link to discover more about you and find a reason to follow you. Avoid linking directly to online marketplaces where people that click can easily click off your page and onto one of your competitors. Instead, link to your own website or your blog.

## Where to link to from your social media profiles

Social media networks will ask you to provide a weblink; some will allow you to add multiple links, but sites such as Twitter give you the option of adding just one link.

So how do you choose which link to add? Most people simply add the main homepage of their website or perhaps a link through to their Etsy shop, but it is worth giving this a little more thought!

Linking to a shop directly means that the first experience your visitor has is being marketed to. If you link to a marketplace, it can also result in the visitor clicking away and finding other shops.

While you want to sell an item, it's unlikely that someone browsing Twitter is in the buying mode. So don't make this the goal – the goal should be to encourage them to follow your updates or sign up to your newsletter. You want them to focus on finding out more about you.

## First impressions count

When someone first lands on a website they make a split-second decision about you and your business. They are either impressed or not!

They will immediately make a decision about whether or not to follow you, whether or not they like what you make or think you are interesting, and whether they want to find out more information about you and your business.

A great idea is to link to specific landing pages on your website or blog for a visitor coming from a social network. This way you can tailor that page to the needs of the visitor.

While your website homepage may be full of all the information that someone searching for a handmade gift needs, the page to which you direct a visitor from one of your profiles can be an extension of your short profile. For example, you might link to an 'About Me' page, where you can add details about your work and your inspirations – and most importantly, add the best images of your work and any accolades, such as where your work has been featured in the past. Keep the information brief and, as always, allow your personality to shine through in your writing.

This kind of information will be sure to pique the interest of a potential new follower. Whether they are a journalist, blogger or potential customer, you need to present the best version of your business on this landing page.

When you measure the traffic coming through from social networks to these links, take a look at the visitor behaviour. Do they tend to click away immediately or do they delve deeper into your site? Learn from their behaviour and the outcomes and adapt the landing page to suit. Keeping this page full of up-to-date information is vital; outdated information could make your business look lacklustre and defeat the object of the page.

# LOGOS AND AVATARS

An avatar is the small image that represents you on social networks. Most businesses use their company logo. Here are some tips for a successful avatar:

» Create a simple, eye-catching avatar

» Use the same avatar across all of your social networks

» Make sure the thumbnail version looks good

» Avatars are small and in most cases text will be unreadable and details in images will be lost. All social networks have help pages detailing the sizes of images for profile pictures and any other images.

» Go for a bold image that stands out.

» Avatars usually need to be square. If your logo isn't, then you need to use a program such as Photoshop or a free version, for example, Gimp (www.gimp.org) to create a square version of your logo. Having half the words cut off looks unprofessional.

» If you aren't good at Photoshop and don't have the time to learn, employ a graphic designer to help you to design your avatar. There are many young or part-time designers just starting out, and they often publicize their services through handmade marketplaces. Always check their feedback or references, and look at examples of their previous work before hiring them.

If you have a great photo of yourself then you could use it as your avatar. A smiling face can be really useful when networking!

# FACEBOOK

Almost everyone has heard of Facebook. Love it or loathe it, Facebook is an extremely useful platform for a creative business to interact with and engage with potential customers and brand advocates.

In this chapter I will explain the basics of Facebook Pages and also the more complex and ever-changing algorithm Facebook uses to decide which posts get seen by whom. I'll also take a look at how you can interact on Facebook for maximum effect. With this understanding, you can create a healthy, active Facebook Page that will build awareness of your brand.

## How can a Facebook Fan Page help grow your business?

Each individual Facebook user sees a unique news feed, personalized for them by Facebook, showing updates from friends, from pages they have liked and from sponsored posts or adverts. Not every update from all of their friends and the brand pages they like will make it into this news feed.

The aim for a Facebook Page manager is to get the pictures, links, news and questions they share on their Facebook Page into the news feed of as many relevant people as possible. It's not necessarily about the number of fans, it's more about how engaged those fans are with the content you share.

Converting a visitor to your website or blog into a Facebook fan is a way of keeping your brand in their minds. Each appearance of your page in their news feed and interaction with your posts strengthens the relationship they have with your brand. It is also a way of amplifying the effect of one visit. You can turn a single website visit into a long-term relationship and you can also access friends of fans, growing your 'reach' to potential new customers exponentially in some cases.

## Facebook Page basics

### Personal Facebook profile
A personal profile is the standard Facebook account designed for an individual person to keep in touch with friends and family who also use Facebook. You can set posts to your Facebook wall to be public or just visible to certain friends, so you can control who sees what.

### Facebook Fan Page
This is an entirely public fan page for businesses where they can build up a following by posting interesting updates for their fans. Search engines can also see information posted on a public Facebook page. When a Facebook user with a personal profile likes your page, they are allowing updates from your page to be part of their news feed.

### Facebook Group
Facebook groups are for communities and clubs that share a common interest and shouldn't really be used for commercial purposes. Only a personal profile can set up and post to a Facebook group.

## KIRSTY ELSON

People often ask me how come I have so many followers on Facebook, and what it boils down to is dedication and hard work! I started my page four years ago and it was a slow burner for a long time, but the more likes you have, the quicker you accumulate more - like a snowball effect. My page likes have more than doubled to over 100,000 in the last three months!

# How to create a Facebook Page

»   All the information you need to set up a Facebook page is contained in Facebook's own help pages. You will first need a personal Facebook profile in order to set up a page. Go to: www.facebook.com

»   If you don't already have a Facebook profile, head to Facebook.com and you will be guided through setting up a personal profile. Don't worry – you don't need to upload any pictures or keep this profile updated if you don't want to. From one Facebook profile you can manage multiple Facebook pages and your profile will always remain private and separate from the page.

»   The next step is to create the page for your brand. Go to: www.facebook.com/pages/create

»   Follow the step-by-step instructions on the 'Create a Page' link – there are just a few steps. You will be given a number of options for the type of business you run and asked to name your page. Choose the one that fits your company best. Do not choose 'local business' if you do not have a public premises where people can visit and buy your crafts.

»   At the time of writing, Facebook only allows you to change the name of your page once, and only if you have fewer than 200 fans. All the other settings, including the page type, can be edited whenever you like, so don't panic if you are not sure to start with.

## What is the news feed?

The news feed is what every Facebook user sees first when they log in – a stream of activity from all the friends and pages they have liked. It is your job as a page manager to get your posts into as many news feeds as possible.

A Facebook friend or fan can do any one of the following things with each item that appears on their news feed. Each activity can in turn create a news feed story that may appear in your friends' or fans' news feeds.

The three main activities that you should look to increase on your Facebook posts are likes, comments and shares; collectively, we call this 'post engagement'.

# Facebook activities

»   **Like**
    When a fan (someone who has liked your page) likes your Facebook post by clicking 'like' beneath it, a 'Facebook story' is created and Facebook may share this in the news feed of the fans' friends. As a result, friends of your fans might come and check out your page and interact with it, creating another story. In this way, the number of stories created can grow exponentially and posts can go viral.

»   **Comment**
    If a fan comments on your post, a story is created and this can be reported as activity in their friends' news feeds. Facebook makes decisions on who to share the story with based on interactions between friends in the past.

»   **Share**
    A fan can like your post so much they share it to their friends or to their fan page. This post can then appear in their fans or friends' news feeds.

## Customizing your news feed

By clicking on the little symbol at the top of every post or hovering over the name of a Facebook Page or friend, a user can make important decisions to control what they are seeing in their news feed.

» **Follow a post**
Without liking, commenting or sharing, you can choose to follow a post or 'get notifications' – to keep an eye on that particular story. No story is created but it's effectively a private way of keeping track.

» **Hide a post – 'I don't want to see this'**
This is when a fan decides they do not want the post to appear in their news feed next time they log in. Facebook will take note of this and may not share future similar posts.

» **Report spam**
Any Facebook fan or friend can report a post as spam. It's obviously not a desirable outcome and can negatively affect your account.

» **Decide to unlike the page or friend that posted it**
It's very easy to unlike a page. If people do this, be sure to look at the post that caused them to make that decision using your Facebook Insights (see later in this chapter). Maybe you went a bit far or maybe you posted too many times that day – were the posts too boring or similar?

» **Get notifications**
By hovering on the page's name and clicking 'like' you can choose to get notifications from a page when a post is added. This means you will never miss a post because Facebook will alert you every time this happens.

### THE ALL-IMPORTANT FACEBOOK NEWS FEED

Facebook's founder, Mark Zuckerberg, uses the words 'real time serendipity' and 'frictionless engagement' when he talks about how he wants people to interact with Facebook. He wants people to enjoy the Facebook experience and all connected apps, but with the average user having many friends and liking many pages, how does Facebook decide which of the 1,500 or more stories to allow into a user's Facebook news feed?

Recently, Facebook has made it quite clear that it gives priority to posts from friends over posts from liked pages in a news feed, so page managers have to work very hard to get posts noticed.

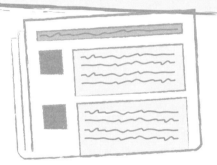

» **Follow/unfollow**
It seems unfair, but Facebook allows users to like a page but not to follow the posts. By choosing Unfollow when hovering on a page's Facebook name, posts will not appear in the user's news feed.

» **Ignore it and keep scrolling**
Users may just scroll past your post, which is not good as you will see when you read about the Facebook Algorithm in 'Making social networking work for you'.

# Facebook post types

» **Status updates**

Any type of post from a user or page on Facebook is known as a status update. Posts come in many different formats.

» **Plain text status update**

This is a text update with no attached link or image. Just write your update in the box and hit 'post'. This is most often used for chatty questions or off-the-cuff news.

» **Status update with a link**

You can paste a link into the status update box at the end of your message. Facebook will automatically create a link image and snippet from the web page. Rather than relying on the link that Facebook automatically chooses, you also have the option to edit the image when posting a link.

» **Photo**

You can upload a photo and add a link and a text description to the post. If the image is not your own, always provide a link to the original source. Facebook is becoming a very visual social network with a large percentage of posts containing images. Within the craft industry, I have found that image posts are often more successful than text posts in terms of engagement as they attract more attention in the news feed.

» **Video**

To share a link to a video, simply paste in the link into the status box. Use the photo/video option only when uploading your own videos. Facebook automatically allows video links to be played within your fans' news feed. They don't need to click the link, just the 'play' symbol.

» **Facebook Event**

You can create a Facebook Event and invite friends to attend through a Facebook Invitation. Facebook will guide you through the set-up process. Your events can be virtual, such as an online sale. Facebook Events are great for sharing details of craft shows or even launching new products. They are a way of reminding people of an important date if you want their support to share and promote it.

> *Facebook Events are great for sharing details of craft shows or even launching new products.*

» **Milestones**

Milestones are placed as important happenings on your timeline – what marks a milestone is entirely up to you. A fun trend is to mark when you reach a certain milestone number of fans on your page or perhaps selling a certain number of orders – anything goes! You can add the date and a photo, so if your company has had interesting milestones in the past, such as the launch of a new range or a feature in a popular magazine, add these in to create interest in your news feed. People love to help you celebrate so milestones can be very popular posts if not overused.

» **Offers**

Offers are links to discounts and deals available to your Facebook fans and need to be paid for. The amount you pay depends on how many of your fans you want to reach. For more details on Facebook advertising, see 'Advertising objectives'.

## Functions and features on Facebook

### Facebook Wall

Every Facebook profile and page has a Facebook Wall. Effectively, this is the homepage where all the posts and images from a user are collected in chronological order.

On Facebook pages, only posts from the page itself are shown on the wall by default, with posts from 'others' appearing in a separate area.

### @Tagging

To tag a photo or an update, you type an @ followed by the name of the page or profile to be tagged. That person or page will automatically be sent a notification and, depending on their settings, your post will appear on their Facebook Wall. It also creates a link within your post that fans can click on to go directly to that page and, if they mouse over the name, they can like that page directly from your page.

Facebook Pages cannot tag a personal profile unless answering a comment by that person on their own Facebook Page post. You can also add tags to other people's updates, even tagging your own page if you are featured in some way in the image.

I find tagging is a really useful tool for involving influential or complementary Facebook pages in a post. But take care with it – overuse will appear spammy.

### Facebook photo albums

Facebook allows you to create photo albums that make it really easy for customers to see what you like (inspiring images, either your own or other people's), what you make, and what you sell and do. You can create an album by clicking on the photo's tab and following the instructions to add photos. You simply upload them from files on your computer.

# Facebook photo albums

» **Include albums of works in progress, events and more**
Your photos can help potential customers really get a feel for your company, making it feel busy and interesting to look around.

» **Be selective**
Only ever share the best images. Don't share 20 slightly different pictures of the same item!

» **Make them relevant**
Add descriptions of the photos and, where appropriate, share a link and tag images with any relevant pages. For example, if you were at a craft fair you could tag these images with stall owners featured.

## Facebook apps and tabs

Every Facebook page can also add apps and tabs in addition to the sections that are added automatically when you create a new page, such as 'About' and 'Photos'.

These tabs/apps can either be static website style pages or apps and services that you have allowed permission to interact with your page - for example you can add a Twitter app which shows all your latest tweets when you click on it, or a Pinterest tab which shows all pins from a certain board.

Use the Facebook app centre to find apps - https://www.facebook.com/appcenter/

With the current Facebook design (which changes regularly!) there is only one custom app visible in the navigation at the top of the page - Timeline, About, Photos, the app of your choice and 'more', which allows people to click to see all of the apps and custom pages you have created. You can rearrange which tab is featured by clicking 'Manage Tabs'.

I would suggest featuring a newsletter sign up page, search for an app in the app centre or, if you are using Mailchimp or another newsletter service, look at their options for integrating Mailchimp with your Facebook page and creating a sign up tab for your fan page.

You can link directly to any tab page or app, and this can be useful for running promotions and competitions where you want people to go to a specific tab on your Facebook page. Search for competitions in the app centre to see all the apps you can use to help with running Facebook competitions.

### The Facebook ticker

The 'ticker' is a constant stream of the very latest activity of your friends and pages you have liked – it sits in the right sidebar. It is only visible when you are logged in to your personal profile and not when you are on a Facebook page. The ticker can be switched on and off very easily by any Facebook user so you can't guarantee your updates will be seen here.

### Scheduling posts

It's very easy to schedule a post on Facebook. You simply write a post then click on the clock symbol in order to add the day and time you want the post to appear. It's good to schedule posts in advance so you have at least one post per day.

*It's good to schedule posts in advance so you have at least one post per day.*

### Hashtags

Adding a hashtag allows your post to be collected together with all other posts with the same hashtag. Click on a Facebook hashtag or use the search function to find all posts tagged with the same hashtag. This can be a useful way of finding pages with similar interests.

**FIONA PULLEN, THE SEWING DIRECTORY**

Just a little tip: you tend to get more reach on Facebook if you post or preschedule direct on Facebook than via a third-party app.

### Targeting posts

You should also see the option to target Facebook posts next to the schedule and tagging symbol when writing a post. You can target the post by gender, language, age, location, relationship and educational status and even sexual preference. The location feature is particularly useful for pages with a global reach where people in different areas use different languages. For a crafter, it can be useful for promoting events – for example, you can tell just your local fans that you'll be at a market the following weekend.

## Understanding the Facebook algorithm

Facebook currently has a very complex algorithm, which makes it one of the most challenging social media networks on which to create a successful account.

Facebook scores each update based on its complex algorithm. It doesn't know you and how much you love what you do – it just sees statistics and interactions. This is why you must focus on engaging fans from the very beginning.

# AFFINITY, WEIGHT AND DECAY

The variables of Affinity, Weight and Decay (which Facebook used to call 'Edge Rank' variables) are a good starting point for understanding the very basic elements of the complex Facebook algorithm.

» **Affinity**
Affinity is dependent on a user's relationship with a story in the news feed – this is based on the user's interaction with similar previous stories. It will also take into account, for example, whether a friend has liked, shared or commented on the story. Facebook learns from people's status updates, profile information and activity on the network. It then shares the story with people it believes have an 'affinity' with your post and are most likely to engage with it.

» **Weight**
Weight is determined by the type of story, such as a photo, video, link or text. On some pages, people tend to like photos from a page more than other types of updates, so Facebook will share the photo posted to one fan, but not the status update posted just a few hours later. This varies though. I manage pages where plain-text updates perform much better than photos and achieve a much greater reach, but on other pages the audience much prefers photos. You will learn more by looking at your Facebook Insights (see later in this chapter).

» **Time Decay**
The last variable is Time Decay. As a story or update gets older, the lower the value – 48 hours is often regarded as the maximum lifespan of a story within a news feed. Viral posts are kept alive through sharing. More recently, Facebook has taken into account the popularity of a story and allowed it to appear in news feeds through continued likes and comments, mentioning the date of the original post next to the 'story'.

*Making social networking work for you*

The algorithm changes and adapts in real time. If fans like or comment on an update very quickly, it will then increase the share of the post to more of your fans and so on. The likes and comments are almost like doors unlocking within your fan count. If an influential and relevant page likes your post this can have a significant impact on a post, unlocking more and more doors!

In my experience the quicker you achieve likes, comments and shares the larger the percentage of users will see your posts. It's almost as if Facebook is testing a batch of your fans, and the number of users it opens the post to is directly determined by this initial batch test.

The interactions on every post then get added back into the big calculator, and the next time you post, it will go to more people. It is suggested that Facebook takes account of the last 50 interactions from a Facebook user, so your page is only as good as your last few dozen posts! This is why it is important to consistently update your page, and only with relevant content.

When a user just scrolls past your update, effectively ignoring your post, Facebook thinks, 'Oh, they didn't think much of that. We'll keep it out of their busy news feed and put this other page in instead next time.'

## When to share on Facebook

When will most of your fans be active online? Luckily, with Facebook's own Insights (available in your Facebook Page admin area) you can find the optimum posting times so you can schedule posts to suit.

Many updates can be scheduled in advance, but you need to reserve time every day, if possible, for live networking. Being available when a post goes live to immediately respond to initial comments can be a great way to create more of a buzz about the content you have just shared.

If you can get to grips with all the ways people can interact with your page, and how to encourage interaction by creating a strategy for sharing great content, you will manage to make the algorithm your friend. Measuring the success of certain post types and also varying post types are key to reaching a larger percentage of your fan base.

Before you start the next section about advanced networking, it is important to create a page and become used to the Facebook platform.

## Networking with complementary business pages

You need to get comfortable with switching between your personal and page profiles on Facebook: use the gear symbol to change from one to the other. Facebook will remind you that you are posting as your page and you will have the option to post as your profile if you would prefer. Sometimes a personal reply is best, especially when you have got to know a person and they will recognize your user name on their Facebook Page post.

Boosting your fan numbers and Facebook fan page engagement is not just about your own updates. Choosing great, relevant content to share is essential to keep fans engaged. However, off-page activity is an equally important way of increasing likes and engagement on your fan page and should not be overlooked.

Log into Facebook as your page. Your page has a news feed made up of all the pages you like or follow, just like the page of a personal Facebook user.

Your fans are watching. Everything you post, like or comment on, both on and off your page, could be seen on both the Facebook ticker and in the news feed of a fan of yours. Use this as a chance to show people how friendly, interesting, funny or amazing your page is. As engagement with your existing fans increases, so does the likelihood they will see your page's activity in their news feed. Here are some tips for making your Facebook Page successful.

## Connect with complementary pages

» Search for pages to like that fit into your target market and complement your own brand. For example, if you make hats then a page that makes handbags of a similar style and quality is a good connection – try to brainstorm ideas for complementary businesses.

» Rather than posting a boring 'hi from your newest liker' on a page wall, comment on one of the existing threads. Join the conversation – don't fly post.

» Try writing a question on a page's post rather than a statement, such as 'Wow, what technique did you use for that?' can help develop your relationship with that page and, more importantly, the fans of that page. Any that have commented on the post will also see the reply you receive.

» By commenting on the content of pages that complement your own products and page, you will be seen by their audience. It's a chance to engage with their fans and build up a potentially beneficial relationship with that company. If a fan page reciprocates your like or comments on your posts, its fans, which also represent your target market, will potentially see this in their tickers and news feeds too.

*Join the conversation – don't fly post!*

» Look at the 'likes' of the pages you view. If the page fits with your target market or the pages your competitors like, you will often find a network of similar pages that you can connect with. Don't like them all – be selective and take time to interact with each page as well as clicking like. If you find a 'honey pot' of great pages to interact with, add them to a 'to network with' list rather than just clicking like or follow.

» Don't like or comment on anything you don't actually like. Be genuine – seek out the stuff that you do like.

» Share content from the complementary pages you have found. It's a great way to get noticed by a page and to get seen in your fans' news feeds. Only share content that you think your fans will really enjoy and don't overdo it.

# Be efficient

» Use keywords to find relevant pages, and sort by 'pages' so you don't waste time scrolling through groups because you cannot join a group as a page.

» Use the 'most recent' option at the top of the page when checking your page's 'home' news feed. This way you can be in the first few to comment/share something from one of your page's likes. Your comment has more chance of being read by the page and the following commenters this way. Come back to the comment later and add more to the conversation.

» Visit your page's activity log, which can be found in the 'manage' drop down of your admin panel – click on 'use activity log'. Everything you do is logged here so you can pick up on your previous interactions and continue the conversation. For example, if you posted 'Good luck at the fair' then you can visit and ask how it went or comment on their next update if you had missed it in your home news feed.

» Always keep in mind your target audience. Some connections you thought would work well may prove to be a waste of time. Don't be afraid to unlike a page if you no longer think the posts are relevant.

## AVOID SPAMMING

» Never spam pages with adverts for your products (unless invited to do so), especially not those of competitors.

» When you are posting as your page you don't need to add a tag to comments – if you do, it can look spammy.

» Don't copy and paste any messages – you are a spammer if you do and Facebook will not appreciate it – remember that it logs all of your activity. Be a sociable and chatty human being and you won't get in trouble for spamming.

» I have one golden rule when it comes to social media networking: 'If it feels spammy, it probably is'. So think twice before you post on other people's Facebook pages.

*Be sociable, give your page a voice of its own and start actively bringing potential customers over to your fan page.*

### Promoting Facebook updates outside of Facebook

You can also promote your Facebook posts on other networks, to build up those initial likes and Comments. On Twitter you might write a tweet to someone:

'@haptree Hi! I just posted a picture of my latest work in progress on Facebook – what do you think? Would love some feedback! http://link.com'

If you work on building connections through your daily networking, you will find people you feel comfortable sharing links with – and there is no need to feel spammy when asking for interaction. Just make sure that if they do comment, you reply.

You can also embed a Facebook post into a blog post or newsletter – this can help to give longevity to a post. Ensure that the post has a 'hook' to grab attention; usually a question works best. Be sociable, give your page a voice of its own and start actively bringing potential customers over to your fan page.

I hope you will begin to see how important it is to have a strategy for sharing on Facebook – just clicking 'share' three times a day is not enough! You need to really work out what makes your audience tick to get those likes and comments.

## FACEBOOK POST LINKS

To find the link to any of your Facebook posts on Facebook, click on the time of the post just beneath your name, the post will open up and you can copy the link from the address bar. The 'embed' option is available using the drop-down arrow on every post, including on other pages' posts. Embedding a post from a complementary page into a blog post is a fantastic way of networking and supporting that page – an action that hopefully will be reciprocated.

## Setting goals

As I have discussed, your goal for each post is for it to 'reach' as many people as possible. Goals to focus on at the early stage (rather than sales or direct traffic) are increasing numbers on an email list and connecting with influencers.

Create a general schedule for your Facebook updates on a simple spreadsheet. This can be extended to include all of your other social media channels. Your schedule needs to be a simple reference guide that prompts you to share certain post types to maximize your page's reach.

Printing your schedule off once a week with some specific goals will give your week's networking a real purpose. It really focuses your efforts based on the themes and goals you have set yourself within your broader strategy and you can tick items off as you go along! For an example of a schedule, see 'Creating a cross-channel content strategy'.

## Facebook advertising

Facebook offers a variety of ways to advertise and offers a great deal of support to advertisers, with many help pages to aid your advertising choices.

You can advertise in a number of ways. The most simple is to pay for a 'boost' – you can do this directly from your page. 'Boosting' means that more people within your fan base and beyond will see the post in their news feed. It can be beneficial to boost posts that are showing higher than average organic reach as this shows that you have a post that is worth spending money on. As the post is already proving popular within the more limited pool of people it has reached, with more exposure it has the potential to do really well, providing a better return on your investment.

Follow this link to get started and explore all the advertising options: www.facebook.com/ads/create/

You will be asked which of the following advertising objectives you want to achieve with your advert. These are the objectives that you should focus on. There are more advanced options for sites with apps.

## EXAMPLES OF SPECIFIC FACEBOOK GOALS

» **Grow Facebook by X number of fans**
With clients I look at estimating percentage growth rather than numbers. This way it's easy to see quickly how you are doing month to month and where you can expect to be in the future, based on your current levels of growth.

» **Like and connect on Facebook with X number of industry influencers per week**
Find a way to build on the relationship, such as inviting them to guest post or creating a mutually beneficial promotion.

» **Click Through Rate (CTR)**
Increase your Click Through Rate for links to your website.

# Advertising objectives

» **Page post engagement**
Reach more people by promoting one of your Facebook posts (similar to a post Boost).

» **Page likes**
Find new fans by advertising your page within the news feed.

» **Clicks to website**
Promote a link to a specific post or product on your website, or your home page to achieve more clicks to a blog post or new product.

» **Event responses**
Get people to your events.

» **Offer claims**
Boost offer reach by emailing users an offer when they sign up to your mailing list and a reminder to take up the offer on a date you choose.

*Facebook tells you the optimum image size you need for certain adverts. Pay heed to this to ensure your ad gets seen.*

## PAYMENT TYPES

The way you pay for Facebook adverts depends on which objective you have chosen. There are four ways to pay within the advertising management area of Facebook.

» **Cost per mille (CPM)**
Paying for the number of people who see your advert in their news feed or elsewhere on Facebook, such as the sidebar.

» **Cost per click (CPC)**
This bid type is best for getting people to click on your ad. You know what you are paying for but your ad will probably be seen by fewer people than if you pay for CPM.

» **Optimized cost per mille (oCPM)**
This bid type is best for showing your ad to the people who are most likely to take action on your ad for example, liking your Page or clicking a link.

» **Cost per action (CPA)**
When available, this bid type is best for getting people to take action on your ad for example, by liking your Page or clicking a link.

## Targeted Facebook ads

Facebook allows you to specifically target people with your adverts, based on their gender, interests and connections. You can also target only people who are connected to your page or only people who are not connected. This can be useful because you don't want to advertise Page like ads to people who already like your page. Alternatively, you may want to advertise an event only to your existing fans.

Before spending any money, you need to work out the value of your objectives. How much is a click or like really worth to you? Perhaps you could you think of a free way to share the post to more people?

One example would be to share the Facebook post on Twitter or Pinterest, or add it to a newsletter sent out directly after you post. This will boost engagement and help improve your reach organically – for free.

# "How do you define success on Facebook"

## Free Facebook promotion

You may find a more pleasant way of advertising is to host a competition, offering a product as a prize. You'll be spending money to boost engagement and help get your page noticed by some new fans as well as being able to promote the give-away across all of your social networks. Remember to take a look at Facebook's latest competition and promotion rules before you run a Facebook competition.

Alternatively, spending time networking with influencers can result in more exposure in the long run. So consider your budget and available time carefully, and make sure your actions fit with your overall strategy.

## Measuring success – Facebook Insights

Facebook has an analytics area called Insights, which you can use to measure your activity and results, looking at reach, the number of engaged users and the virality of your posts. You can look at posts within set dates and sort them by which had the most comments, or most likes. You will soon see which posts are working for you.

This is a link to the help area for Facebook Insights. Read through the guides, which will help to explain how to start to use Insights effectively. Go to www.facebook.com/help and navigate to the Insights page.

# Facebook Insights terms

» **Likes**
The number of new people who have clicked like and can potentially see your updates

» **Reach**
How many people could potentially have seen your post in their news feed

» **Engagement**
Likes and comments (these also have a direct effect on reach)

» **CTR**
These are Click Through Rates (the number of people who click through from your Facebook post links to your blog or website), found from your Google analytics.

» **Talking about**
How many stories were created around your page from interactions, likes, events and more.

*You may need to set more modest, achievable goals to ensure the time you spend on Facebook is worthwhile.*

However, more important than the statistics Facebook provides within Facebook Insights are the results of your own networking goals, week to week or month to month. Did you achieve them? Did you create any new sales leads and interact with any new influencers? If not, why not? What held you back?

If lack of time is always the main reason why you have not achieved your set goals, then you need to reassess the goals you are setting and your systems – are they realistic? You may need to set more modest, achievable goals to ensure the time you spend on Facebook is worthwhile.

# PINTEREST

Pinterest is like an online manifestation of the traditional pile of coffee-table books we like to have on display in our homes. They are books that look gorgeous inside and out, filled with amazing images, projects we are working on, or would be if we had the time or the skills, and destinations we are planning to visit. They're books and magazines that make us and our friends go 'Ooooh', spark up a conversation and give us aspirations to work towards.

## How can a Pinterest account help grow your business?

Pinterest can drive a lot of traffic to your website, even if you don't have a Pinterest account! This is because it allows us to bookmark and share images and websites on 'boards' – just like having a series of pinboards full of memos and magazine clippings. Our Pinterest boards not only project our tastes and passions but can also be a useful way of filing great resources that we need right now or will read later on.

People use Pinterest as a visual search engine – they look for inspiration for their latest projects and products to add to their wish lists. When you follow someone on Pinterest, their pins show up on your home page along with all the other pinners you are following – just like the Facebook news feed but laid out in a grid.

You can search Pinterest to find pins on certain subjects. It's a great resource for finding relevant content to share on your other networks and can be excellent as inspiration for blog posts about your particular subject for your specific target market.

## FREE RESEARCH

If you follow the right people or Pinterest boards, then Pinterest is like having a team of people doing your research for you. They are working for you for free, finding useful and interesting resources with the most beautiful images, and all on your chosen niche subject.

No other social media sites allow you to follow just one aspect of a person or company's interest – Pinterest does! If you sew, you can follow just the sewing boards of hundreds of people, cutting away all the other pins they share and just allowing your news feed to be constantly updated with sewing posts.

## Pinterest basics

Work your way through the Pinning 101 contents on Pinterest's help page. It explains the basics of pinning and how to use the Pin it Bookmarklet. It really is helpful to understand the 'anatomy' of a pin and Pinterest board.

### Business or personal page?
A business page is best if you are serious about building your brand. There is currently not a big difference between the business and personal accounts, other than the option to verify your website and the ability for business pages to create widgets to add to your website and blogs. This difference may well change in the future as Pinterest develops the business side and adds more ways of building revenue.

If you already have a personal Pinterest page, you can convert it to a business page, so you needn't lose any existing followers. For details on Pinterest for businesses go to http://business.pinterest.com/

## MAGGY WOODLEY, RED TED ART

For me, Pinterest created a step change in traffic flow. My site RedTedArt.com was doing well. But when Pinterest arrived it grew to more than six times its size in a matter of months. It changed everything. It even changed the way I blogged. I started to focus on my 'best photos possible'. I made them bigger and better.

### Pinning tactics – networking on Pinterest

Starting to pin for your business is a bit like standing in a room made of cork boards, being handed a packet of pins, a pair of scissors and 60 million magazines and being asked to decorate them. Where do you start? You need a strategy! What do you want your room to say about you and your business that will make people want to hang out in there?

You need a strategy!

### What is your target audience searching for online?

The content we share needs to 'fit' and complement our target market. We need to filter out noise and focus on goals.

It may not be a person searching for your exact product, but you want them to find you and follow your boards because you share images, links and videos that interest them – the basic principle of good content marketing! Remember the ABC method discussed in 'Is social networking worth your time and energy?' This is the acquisition phase – bringing the right people to you.

### The Pinterest Bookmarklet

See the help area on Pinterest for details of how to install the 'pin it' widget. With this widget installed in your browser, pinning will become second nature for you. It takes seconds to pin an image, and the link is automatically attached. You just click the icon in your toolbar and the images you can pin on any website pop up. You pick the image, pick which board you want to add the image to and then add a little text.

As you are researching blog posts, Twitter and Facebook and looking through your RSS feeds for content to share, you will naturally find images and videos that fit your niche topics. Use Pinterest as a tool to collect up all the fantastic blog posts you find while you are searching the Internet for inspiration.

### Pinterest boards

Create boards on various niche elements of your subject. The text you use to describe a board will help people to decide whether or not to follow your board. At the SEO level, you want your boards to appear in search engines for subjects your target market may be searching for.

Boards should be submitted to a particular category – you can select the category by clicking on 'edit board'.

# PRACTICAL NETWORKING TIPS

» Try not to pin to just one board at a time in quick succession because this can flood people's Pinterest news feeds.

» Try to pin throughout the day, grabbing the opportunities as they arise when you are online.

» Try to mix up the number of repins, pins from web pages and original pins uploaded by you.

» Always ensure the pin links to the original source and not to a spam or fake link.

» Try not to pin from a home-page address – link to the blog post's link. In a few weeks it will become hard for anyone to find the original image from the home page of a blog or regularly updated website. This is annoying!

» Where there is a choice of similar images to pin, go for the one with the largest dimensions. Pinterest shows you the sizes when you click 'pin it' or use the Pinterest widget.

» Regularly search for new people and brands to follow and engage with.

» Take care and be selective with who to follow. You want your home page to be full of highly relevant Pinterest users all acting like your personal marketing team, finding you juicy content to share.

» Create a list of board ideas as part of your social media schedule. You want your boards to be active and busy to encourage new followers.

» There is no rush to fill a board! Quality takes priority over quantity every time.

» Promote your Pinterest boards and share your latest pins on other networks.

### Themes, titles and descriptions for Pinterest boards

Keep up with your Pinterest housework. The goal is to get people repinning your content in order to reach out to new Pinterest users.

### Keywords – what are people searching for?

Use relevant keywords, but don't write too much. Your text and image should be a teaser to tempt people to click. Always remember that a search engine will use the text – think SEO!

*Your text and image should be a teaser to tempt people to click.*

Keywords enable users to find your Pinterest boards and pins from internal and external searches. As with all content, think hard about the sort of search terms people will be using to find information on the Internet. Will they be looking for colour and texture as well as the type of image?

If you are uploading images, ensure they are named files with descriptive keywords as names rather than numbers your camera or computer has automatically assigned them.

### Hashtags

Add a relevant hashtag. Hashtags become hyperlinks to a search of the word tagged, just like on Twitter and Facebook.

## Building traffic to your website through Pinterest

Creating boards and pinning lots of interesting stuff is a brilliant way to help with brand identity. You can give off a wonderful brand image and spend ages preening your boards to absolute perfection.

However, the real traffic you can draw from Pinterest comes not from your activity on Pinterest (particularly if you are new to it) but the activity of people pinning from your site or blog.

### Add a 'Pin It' button beside your images

Make it easy for people to pin your images by adding the 'pin it' button to all of your images – details can be found here: http://business.pinterest.com/en-gb/pin-it-button

Even if your blog readers have added the easy-share Pinterest Bookmarklet to their browser toolbars, the 'pin it' sign reminds them to pin, like a call to action.

In order to add the hover-over 'Pin It' buttons onto your images, you need to add a little code to your website. All the details are in the widget builder area of the Pinterest for Business 'tools' section of the site.

## Make your content more pinnable

You need to optimize your blog-post images for Pinterest users. Only use high-quality images on your blog and website. There are lots of photography tips on the Craft Blog UK website that will help you get your photography up to scratch.

Adding high-quality, beautiful images to your blog content could mean your posts are picked up and shared on Pinterest by its army of social media-loving users. This could potentially see your post spread across Facebook and Twitter too, so it's worth spending time choosing the right images to accompany your blog post text.

### Add text to your original images

You can use simple, free editing software to add text to an image – most software gives you this option, for example Pic Monkey (www.picmonkey.com), which is really user friendly and very popular with bloggers. Alternatively, download Gimp, a free version of Photoshop, if you want more flexibility with fonts.

### 'Click Me' text

When you add text, it should be enough to make people realize that if they click they will get something like a tutorial or a list of top tips. A Pinterest browser would not know just by looking at an image that it linked to a turorial or a collection of tips rather than a finished product, and they won't always read the text beneath each image. Just the word DIY or Top Tips can be enough to pique interest and get people to click through to your post. Remember that Pinterest users love beautiful things, so make sure the picture is lovely enough to carry the text. Choose your fonts and font sizes carefully to fit your brand image.

> Remember that Pinterest users love beautiful things, so make sure the picture is lovely enough to carry the text.

Try using the same careful treatment on your leading images with every post. People will begin to recognize your unique style – your brand identity. When they are presented with the choice of which image to pin they will naturally be drawn to the image with text as it saves them time describing the pin.

Even if you are yet to set up a website, you can link images through to your Facebook page, to albums of your work in progress or work for sale – just click 'edit' on the pin once you have uploaded the image and paste in the link to your Facebook page. Every Pinterest image you upload this way needs to have a link attached.

## Building up a Pinterest following

Just as with any other social network, you can like and comment on people's pins and follow people. You can also find people from your existing networks, through your email account and networks, and invite them to join or follow you on Pinterest. As your social media networks grow, revisit these links to be sure that people are following you on Pinterest too.

Note that few people comment on Pinterest, so I believe it's worth the effort if you are looking to connect with a particularly influential Pinterest user. You will stand out to them by commenting and not simply repinning.

Other than through using Pinterest's internal search for pins, people or boards, you can discover influential pinners via Twitter or Facebook since many people connect their accounts to these networks. Remember to look out for the Pinterest symbol on blogs and websites.

Pin profiles also include links to people's other networks, so if you find someone whose boards you think are great, check if they have Twitter or a Facebook page and be sure to tell them you like their boards. It could be the start of a great conversation and win you a new Pinterest, Facebook and Twitter follower.

### Competitions

Running competitions will boost follower numbers on social networks, and Pinterest is a particularly good place to get people interested. Make sure you are not just giving things away for free; you need to work out what represents a good return on your investment (ROI).

The competition needs to be fairly straightforward to enter, and the prize should be worth the time it takes. You also need to be able to track entries – consider how you will find entries and make this clear in the competition rules. For example, they might have to repin a particular image, use a specific unique hashtag on their own pins or create a board with a specific name you can then search for.

Be very clear about what the competitors need to do to enter and also the goal of the competition.

## IDEAS FOR COMPETITION ENTRY REQUIREMENTS

» **Repin a pin you have created to enter**
» **Comment on a pin to enter**
» **Pin something from your website or blog and add a hashtag**
» **Create a board on a certain theme to be judged**
» **Create a wish list within a certain budget**

### Creating and joining community boards

Community boards have far greater potential reach than individual boards. The owner of the board invites fellow pinners to contribute to their board. You can do this by clicking 'edit' when on a board and pasting in either the email address or name of one of the pinners you follow. This person will then be notified of the invitation and can accept or decline the offer.

Many of the pinners on my 'Craft Life' board have just a handful of followers, but when they pin to this board they reach thousands of Pinterest users. Community boards are a great way to have your account discovered and to build up followers as well as potentially driving more traffic to your website.

Get together with your existing networks and start your own niche community board. This will certainly help to boost your follower numbers. Inviting someone to pin to a community board also gives you a reason to contact them and build up your online relationship.

If you find a community board you'd like to join, get in touch with the owner of the board. Most people have a website, Facebook or Twitter link on their profiles. It can be tricky to find these community boards since there is no specific search function (at the time of writing), but you can spot community boards through the 'group' symbol in search results and on the community board you will see the contributors listed at the top.

When you find a Pinterest user you like, look at their boards, and if they are a member of community boards that fit your niche, leave a comment asking for them to add you. Even if it's not their board, they should be able to add you as a contributor.

## MAGGY WOODLEY, RED TED ART

One of the reasons I was able to benefit from Pinterest so quickly was through networking and collaborating with other bloggers. Networking wasn't a conscious decision, it was more about connecting with my fellow bloggers and establishing friendships and working relationships. These relationships gave me access to so-called 'collaborative' boards - other pinners would invite me to pin to their already big and established boards.

## Measuring success on Pinterest

Success on Pinterest can be judged by the number of followers you have and by looking at your analytics to see how much traffic is being sent to your website through your pinning and that of others.

To find out if your website content has been pinned you can use the following link: http://pinterest.com/source/ukcraftblog.com/ Replace my address, ukcraftblog.com, with your website (or any site) and see whether or not people are already pinning your images.

Pinterest also has its own analytics feature. You can see interesting basic data that tells you at a glance which pins are doing well in terms of being repinned and which are bringing the most clicks through to your website.

You need to verify your website for the in-house Pinterest analytics feature to work. You can do this by adding a snippet of code to your blog or website. The link is:

http://blog.pinterest.com/post/34315137913/verifying-your-website

The Pinterest analytics feature is quite basic so I tend to focus on using Google Analytics to track success on Pinterest.

# TWITTER

Twitter is a microblogging site where people can post updates in no more than 140 characters – effectively the length of one sentence. It is popular as a way to keep in touch with friends and brands, make new friends and to keep up to date with what people are talking about in general, around certain subjects or within a niche group.

## How can a Twitter account help grow your craft business?

Many companies use Twitter purely as another arm of their customer service team. Important as interacting with customers can be, Twitter can be so much more, especially in the early days when you are building your online presence.

You can use Twitter to network with industry experts and influencers on a level playing field, regardless of the number of followers you have, creating connections that can have a stratospheric effect on your craft business.

It doesn't take long to get the hang of tweeting. Within a week of starting your Twitter account, you will be RT-ing and @ing like a professional! The best way to learn is to get onto the site, begin clicking and finding your way around, and start writing tweets.

*Within a week of starting your Twitter account, you will be RT-ing and @ing like a professional!*

### PATRICIA VAN DER AKKER, THE DESIGN TRUST

I am a big fan of Twitter, and I use it daily to promote and interact with our audience. On Twitter I answer questions, give practical business info, retweet useful info or images I like. Many tweets have a link back to blog posts, so Twitter drives about 70 per cent of our traffic, which is extremely important as we can then develop a further and deeper relationship with our audience. It's important that you create your own voice, that you show up consistently, and that you focus on being helpful to your audience. I have steadily created a huge Twitter following in the last two years, and our profile wouldn't have risen so much if it hadn't been for Twitter.

# Twitter basics

The following are a few basic terms that you need to understand. Twitter has an extensive help section that you may also find helpful when starting out:https://support.twitter.com/

» **Twitter stream**
When you are on your Home page you will see a stream of all the tweets posted by people you are following. This is all their tweets, not just those addressed to you. The more people you follow, the busier this feed gets and the more interesting and useful. Once you are following more than 100 or so people it can be difficult to keep up, which is why you should create Twitter Lists.

» **Tweet**
Any update on Twitter is a tweet.

» **@**
Using the @ symbol you can add someone's name to a tweet so that they will be notified of the tweet. Regularly check your @connect tab to see if people are talking to you and be sure to reply to any tweets directed at you.

» **Reply**
Click Reply on a tweet and you begin to create a conversation thread. The @name of the person who tweets is automatically included at the beginning of your reply.

» **Retweet/RT**
Click Retweet to share someone else's tweet with your own followers.

» **Modified tweet/MT**
This is when you retweet but slightly change the tweet. This is useful if you want to add your own message but don't have enough space – you can simply delete part of the original tweet.

» **Direct message/DM**
Sometimes you want your tweet to someone to be private. You can only Direct Message (DM) someone who is following you. Don't spam people's inboxes, only DM someone for genuine reasons when you want to get in touch but don't want your tweet to be public. Occasionally I will DM a Twitter contact that I have already built up a relationship with on Twitter or elsewhere, to let them know about a new post that I think they will really be interested in (and may be inclined to share).

» **#Hashtag**
If you add a hashtag to a word, the word appears as a hyperlink and when clicked will bring up on Twitter a stream of every tweet that uses this tag. Try searching #handmade or #craft, for example. Hashtags are also used in Tweet Chats, where groups get together and chat at the same time on a certain topic.

» **Twitter Lists**
These are lists of Twitter users, and can be public (seen by your followers) or private only to you.

» **Favourite**
If you add a tweet to your favourites, other Twitter users will get a notification of this so it's a nice way to show your appreciation for another Twitter user. You can also create widgets from Favourite tweets.

» **Twitter widgets**
Twitter widgets can be placed on your website to give your readers a snippet of your activity or to encourage them to follow you. See https://twitter.com/settings/widgets

## Twitter etiquette

Twitter is as high brow or low brow as you make it, from the importance of Pushkin in the golden era of Russian literature, to the latest news from a war zone, to what Cheryl Cole had for breakfast. If you don't like someone's opinion, unfollow them. Don't ever get embroiled in a Twitter dispute because it will be bad for your professional reputation.

I have seen many people 'get personal' on Twitter. As with all your social networking, remember at all times to keep your account professional and true to your brand.

Beware of appearing like a spammer. Not every tweet should be an advert or contain a link to your own sites. There are many Twitter applications that can be used to analyse people's tweets; they give the ratios of tweets containing links, allowing the user to filter out spammers. For example, www.klout.com gives a score to rate your influence in certain areas.

Most people are understanding of links to new listings and blog posts spread through the day, because of course you want to catch a few different time zones – especially if you don't want to post and run but instead take time to interact with other users. It's only if every single tweet is promotional or scheduled that your Twitter feed becomes anti-social.

Remember to say thank you when someone follows you, retweets or shares one of your tweets. It gets trickier to find time to do this as your following grows, but in the early days it's really important to use these small interactions as conversation starters.

# TWITTER NETWORKING - FROM FOLLOW TO SALE!

Imagine these two Twitter accounts start to follow my account. I see their bios pop up in my Twitter notifications. Both have found me because I've recently followed a fashion blogger they follow.

@ AmysJewels - I am a mother of two who makes and sells jewellery in her spare time. I have a shop on Etsy if you want to see my work.

@ JemmaLeeDesigns - Hi I'm Jemma, a mum, jewellery designer and fashion addict! If you crave pretty & shiny things you may find my Twitter feed far too tempting!

The first profile makes me think that a bored housewife is going to be constantly tweeting what she has for sale on Etsy. I'm immediately switched off by the idea of this and don't follow her back or bother to look at her recent tweets.

The second sounds more vibrant and chatty – she sounds sociable and she's a designer, which is cool! She's a mum, something I can relate to, but also a fashion lover like me. I'm intrigued by the bio so I'll have a look at her tweets and find out more. I also now notice she retweeted one of my tweets from yesterday.

I see some really interesting fashion tweets and that Jemma's really chatty with other Twitter users so I decide to follow her back. She responds by thanking me for following and asking me if I'm also a fellow fashionista – we have a brief Twitter convo about my drab wardrobe.

She retweets one of my posts the following day. The next day I see one of her tweets about her latest product launch. By this time I feel really familiar with her avatar and username. I click through to her site to take a look.

At no point did she try and sell to me, yet with a few tweets I'm at her site. I can't afford the jewellery, sadly, but instead I share her link with my followers:

'This ring from @ JemmaLeeDesigns is on my Christmas list – isn't it gorgeous? http://link.com'

Naturally, she thanks me in another tweet and favourites the post, and she adds me to her private 'leads to follow up' Twitter list.

We exchange a few more tweets. For example, she mentions me when sharing her latest blog on 'Brightening up your wardrobe'. I visit her fab blog post and see more of her lovely jewellery in her blog's sidebars. She also joins in a conversation I'm having with another Twitter friend and adds some interesting points.

A week later, she sends me a DM: 'Hi Hilary, I wanted to let you know in advance that I'm having a sale this weekend, but you can use the special code HP10% in advance for 10% off.' I feel like I've got special treatment from a lovely jewellery designer. I'm also worried the one-of-a kind ring may sell on the weekend. I'm compelled not to wait until Christmas and I buy the ring there and then, and I tweet about it.

Of course, it doesn't always work out that way but I hope you can see the value that every aspect of your networking on Twitter has, from your bio, your tweets, your conversations and, most importantly, how you manage information. In this example, Jemma targeted me because I had shown an interest in fashion. With some simple networking, she created a sales lead that she was able to 'keep warm' and follow up when the time was right.

*Making social networking work for you*

## Powerful search and Twitter tools

Twitter is an excellent social media network for connecting with other businesses and finding your niche markets. It is also an extremely useful companion to all of your other social networking activities and I want you to fully grasp its potential.

The first myth I want to clear up is that you need to have thousands of followers to make Twitter work for you. Wrong! Of course, it is good to have many followers – see later in this chapter for my tactics to boost follower numbers. However, Twitter has many benefits that do not rely purely on how many followers you have.

# HOW TWITTER WILL BENEFIT YOUR CREATIVE BUSINESS

## 1. As a research tool for finding your target market audience

Twitter has a great search function, which is always available in the top bar or you can click on 'discover'. You can use 'search' to discover other people's tweets. You can also search by keywords and phrases to find exactly the right people you should be chatting to and encouraging to follow you.

Don't pounce on Twitter users who mention something you are listening for in a Twitter search – this is really spammy. Instead, create a Twitter List (see later in this chapter) of these people, reply to another of their tweets and follow them at a later date. This slower approach will create more engaged followers.

If you have identified that a user is in your target market, it is worth your time to tweet to them. This also helps prevent you from being perceived as a spammer. Your Twitter Lists can be private, so no one needs to know – they should feel it is a serendipitous connection! My clients have had emails from new customers with whom I've networked on their behalf saying 'how lovely it is to tweet to you'.

## ADVANCED SEARCH TECHNIQUES

Twitter has some very clever search tools – use the advanced search from your home page to quickly search for Twitter users in your target market: https://twitter.com/search-advanced. Several of these search techniques also work when using search engines such as Google.

Here are some examples that I might use to find crafters to follow. When the searches are returned, Twitter uses 'top', 'all' or 'people you follow' to refine the results. Using a combination of these search operators can be extremely useful for pinpointing who to follow and who to add to lists based on what they have been tweeting about.

| TYPE INTO SEARCH BAR | FINDS TWEETS... |
|---|---|
| craft blog | containing both 'craft' and 'blog'. This is the standard search which most people use. By using the advanced searches below you can really tailor your results. |
| 'craft blog' | containing the exact phrase 'craft blog' – useful to find people talking about an exact phrase |
| craft OR blog | containing either 'craft' or 'blog' (or both). A wide search of terms. |
| craft -beer | containing 'craft' but not 'beer'. Removing a term with the minus symbol is very useful. There is a brand of beer called craft beer and obviously these tweets are not relevant for me, so by removing beer, I just find the craft tweets. |
| #cbuk | containing the hashtag 'cbuk'. Take a look – this is the Craft Blog UK hashtag and you will be able to see all the latest craft bloggers' tweets. |
| from:haptree | sent from person 'haptree' |
| to:craftbloguk | sent to person 'craftbloguk' |
| @Creativeuni | referencing person 'creativeuni'. If you now sort by 'people you follow', you can see who in your network is also chatting to them – really useful so you can build on relationships. |
| 'craft blog' near:London' | containing the exact phrase 'craft blog' and sent near 'London'. This one is great for finding people in your local area. |
| near:London within:15mi | sent within 15 miles of 'London' |
| crafty since:2013-12-27 | containing 'crafty' and sent since date '2013-12-27' (year-month-day) |
| crafty until:2014-12-27 | containing 'crafty' and sent up to date '2014-12-27' |
| Craft -beer :) | containing 'craft', but not 'beer', and with a positive attitude |
| Blogger :( | containing 'blogger' and with a negative attitude |
| blogging ? | containing 'blogging' and asking a question |
| 'craft blog' filter:links | containing 'craft blog' and linking to URLs |

## 2. Keep up to date with your creative sector

Being active on Twitter and keeping abreast of the tweets sent by influencers within your market will help your company to stay up to date with market trends.

Networking with fellow artists and crafters may not directly lead to sales but it will help kickstart your network if you follow and interact with their accounts. It's easier to encourage new fans and followers once you already have a little network of people to chat to. You can then build up a community vibe and spend more time focusing on networking specifically with your target market in mind.

Share and retweet industry news to your followers, and create conversations around news and events by asking questions or offering opinions. A bricks and mortar shop that is full of interested people milling around gives off a great impression to passersby. That's the effect you are going for, but an online version!

*Advanced search example*

Let's say I want to post details of a social media workshop for creatives happening in London and want to attract Etsy sellers in particular.

I could search 'etsy.com/listing' near:'London', which would bring up people near London sharing Etsy listing links – useful for me because I can tweet them and let them know about the event. That's just one example – think of how many searches you could carry out to really hone in on your own niche market, using all the keywords you have been identifying for your brand. The trick is to stay clear of general search terms, which will bring less relevant users.

## 3. Network with complementary businesses

Use Twitter to interact with businesses that you may be able to work with in the future to build up relationships that could lead to cross promotions. For example, someone selling aprons, tea towels and cafetière cosies may benefit from networking with a cupcake business or a potter.

Incorporate business-to-business networking into your weekly social media strategy – set aside time and work on finding really good complementary businesses with Twitter searches. Look out for Twitter icons on blogs you follow and create niche lists that focus on certain business types.

By engaging on Twitter and letting people know you enjoy their site, you have made the first step. As you build up a rapport, for example, interacting with businesses on their networks, commenting on blog posts and retweeting their content, you can let them know about your latest news without worrying about looking spammy. They'll recognize you and will probably be happy to share your work or accept an offer to work with them on a cross promotion.

> *Share and retweet industry news to your followers, and create conversations around news and events by asking questions or offering opinions.*

## 4. Network with influential publishers/bloggers

This is perhaps one of the most useful aspects of being active on Twitter when you are getting started. Identifying and networking with publishers is a quick way to get your work discovered.

Search for blogs and on and offline magazines in your niche market using Google and Twitter searches. You can also use blog directories and ask in forums to find relevant blogs for your particular market.

Follow the blogger on Twitter or create a Twitter list of bloggers to network with in the future. Set aside time in your weekly social media strategy for engaging with these bloggers. For example, you could assign 10 minutes per week for searching for new blogs and 10 minutes per week for sending out tweets and engaging with these influencers.

The goal is up to you. It could be to get press coverage, have your work shared to create links back to your blog or just to connect, get followed and ask if you could send over an email or add the blogger to your mailing list.

## 5. Build direct traffic to your website

Once you begin to increase follower numbers and you are networking with followers in your niche market, you should begin to see clicks through to your web pages and blog posts from the links you post. You can measure these clicks through analytics installed in your websites or, if you use a URL, shortening service such as http://bit.ly, you can track the click-through rate from this site.

Don't be disappointed by lacklustre click through rates (CTRs) early on. The reality is that you need lots of followers, or lots of people to retweet your updates. Don't focus on this aspect of twitter, focus on building up relationships and ensuring you are following and interacting with relevant twitter users.

### RIN HAMBURGH INSIDE SCOOP

I'm always on the look-out for new ideas, stories, case studies and experts to feature, whether I'm out browsing at a craft market or flicking through a magazine. But my first port of call is always Twitter, especially if I'm on a tight deadline or need someone really specific. I'll tend to use the hashtag #journorequest to flag up my requirements, and then I'll often find that other Twitter users will either retweet or recommend someone, copying in their Twitter handle, so I can reach a far wider audience than just my followers. I've found dozens of crafters this way. The key to being selected is to make sure your profile page is well branded, that you're interacting with the right people, that you come across as an expert and, of course, follow as many relevant journalists as you can - and keep your eye out for that #journorequest hashtag.

I have had tweets retweeted by huge accounts with hundreds of thousands of followers and it's just resulted in a handful of actual clicks through to the link - suggesting their audience is not engaged with them, they don't value the retweets enough to click through. Conversely, I have had tweets shared by smaller accounts from niche bloggers and seen huge engagement through clicks and retweets.

The actual text and subject matter in your tweet is hugely important in order to get people to click a link you have added. Sometimes, simple ideas work. For example, I found that adding 'Don't you think!?' to the end of a tweet increased clicks and replies!

If you aren't measuring, you aren't marketing. You need to work on the quality of your tweets and find out what works for your own audience by measuring your results.

## 6. Run promotions and competitions

One of the great aspects of social media networking is the ability for people to share your updates. Running promotions, give-aways and competitions is a great way to encourage organic sharing of your posts.

Think very clearly about the goal of any Twitter promotion. Is it to build follower numbers or to send traffic to your website? What will be the return on your investment? How will you encourage people to share?

An example of a Twitter competition is to offer an entry to everyone who retweets an update. Professional competition sites can pick these up (using Twitter searches). You will then find that although your link may be tweeted it does not reach the right audience, and the Follows and retweets are fairly pointless and sometimes temporary.

Often, asking people to do something and to engage a little more can bring you a more suitable selection of entrants that will stay with your brand. For example, you could ask them to visit your site and then send out a tweet about their favourite product, mentioning you personally. This way, rather than merely retweeting the link, the person has to actively visit your website and search for products. You can reply to their tweets, so that the interaction becomes very conversational.

One of the most useful applications of social media is to build up your email lists for sending out newsletters. We can never guarantee that Twitter, Facebook or any other network will still be live tomorrow, but emails are much more direct and the list belongs entirely to you. Where possible, incorporate signing up to your newsletter into any competition entry rules.

## 7. Embed tweets

Along with Facebook, Pinterest and Instagram you can embed a post on Twitter into your website or blog. Click on the drop-down arrow on the post, click 'embed tweet', and the code you need to add to your website or blog post will be displayed. When you paste in the code, the post will show, including all the clickable ways to interact with that post, such as favouriting and retweeting.

This is a great way to get people who read your blog engaged in your social networking activity. Use the post as an opportunity to ask a question or as an example of feedback on a certain subject. You can create entire blog posts around one tweet – it doesn't have to be your own, you can embed any tweet into your posts.

I've used the 'embed tweet' function to great effect when asking people to share a post to enter a draw. People can share there and then from your post, and they also see that others are sharing too – great 'social proof' for getting others involved.

# TWITTER FOLLOWERS

If I follow you, it means I get to see your tweets on my home page along with all the tweets of everyone else I follow in chronological order. Following does not have to be reciprocated. You can see the number of people you are following and those who follow you in the top left of your home screen, and these statistics are publicly available.

Quality and not quantity counts with Twitter followers. Followers who regularly chat to you, and retweet your tweets and links to their own followers, are only earned through building relationships with other tweeps (a word for Twitter users).

You need to join in the conversations and be active if you want people to act on your tweets and to be engaged with your content.

It's nice to tweet a quick hello to new followers. Being courteous and friendly (not fawning) is important but don't worry, you are not expected to keep up with every follower!

## UNFOLLOWING

There will come a point when you need to unfollow people in order to follow new people who may be more engaged with your tweets. If you find you are following too many people and they are not following back, this indicates that they aren't interested in your updates. You can use various sites to identify and unfollow people who are not following back or whose accounts are inactive. Try http://iunfollow.com/ or search online for other 'unfollow Twitter' tools.

# Getting more Twitter followers

» **Use your existing networks**
Initially, to increase the number of followers, you can look to any networks you already belong to first. Writing a blog post and letting Facebook fans and friends in forums know you have a Twitter account is a great way of immediately starting off a network of Twitter friends you can chat to and engage with. Having these known connections is useful to give credibility to your account, so people can see you are not a spammer but a genuine Twitter user.

» **Find friends**
Twitter has a 'find friends' function: https://twitter.com/activity. It will search your email contacts and find matching Twitter addresses. This is useful for connecting with customers or users on your mailing lists. While it's good to find new followers, connecting with your existing network on Twitter is extremely useful for building up a highly engaged account. In order to quickly increase your following, you need to follow other Twitter users, who may follow you back.

» **Similar accounts**
Looking at accounts that you feel are similar to yours and following their followers or using the Twitter searches will help you find people to follow. Twitter offers lots of recommendations in its 'Who to Follow' list, but you don't have to follow them all!

» **Celebrities and big businesses**
There are Twitter users with huge followings that follow nobody, but these are normally established celebrities or businesses. Be careful not to get flagged as a spammer by following too many people
» at once. Twitter checks the ratio of followers to following and has a way of detecting spammy activity.

> *In order to increase your following quickly, you need to follow other Twitter users, who may follow you back.*

## Engage with new followers

I'd suggest you leave a week at least after you decide to follow someone to see if they will follow you back. If they do, try to engage with them straight away. Commenting on a new follow is a great way to begin networking.

It's important to try to identify the right people to follow in the first place, which will increase the chances of being followed back.

For example, you might tweet to a new account you are following: '@photographa Just followed and had a look at your site, really like your macro photography – look forward to your tweets!'

This kind of tweet shows you are a real person, and while you are starting to build your following, these personal interactions work extremely well to garner new followers. You could also ask questions, as long as they sound genuine. If you feel you can't be genuine, it's unlikely the person is in your niche market!

Once someone recognizes you are real and haven't spam followed them, they will be much more inclined to engage and follow – and that's the goal of your actions on Twitter.

> *After your tweet chat, retweet posts you think are of interest.*

## Join in tweet chats

Joining a tweet chat is a great way to network and build followers who you know are interested in the same subjects. Click on the Twitter chat hashtag and ensure you have 'all' checked so that you don't just see highlights but a real conversation stream.

Tweet chats usually last 30 minutes to an hour and the people who join the chat all follow a hashtag. I occasionally run a tweet chat with the hashtag #cbuk. It has been immensely popular and although it is fast paced and sometimes hard to keep up, the benefit you will receive from finding lots of like-minded people on Twitter with the same questions as you is fantastic!

When in a tweet chat, make an effort to follow and chat to as many different people as possible. This will increase your number of mentions and the reach to all of the followers of these accounts.

## Twitter Lists

It's easy to add someone to a Twitter List and this can be a public or private list. Just click on the gear icon to find lists and the option to 'Create new list'.

When you are viewing a Twitter profile, there is a little drop-down area next to the Follow button where you can add someone to a list. You don't need to follow them to add them to a list, so this can be useful for keeping an eye on the competition.

You can click on the list at any time and you will cut out all the other noise and only see updates from this select group of Twitter accounts – perfect for creating lists of high-profile people within your industry.

You can use Twitter lists to create targeted streams of relevant information that you can share with your own followers or retweet. The time spent creating and evolving these lists will not be wasted – you are creating a goldmine of useful information that can be retweeted or used in blog posts.

## Sharing content on Twitter

One of the things people find most tricky is finding inspiration for things to share with their followers. Often people tend to just share their own links. It's a good idea to have a bank of interesting content resources. See 'Creating a cross-channel content strategy' for ideas. Sharing interesting and relevant content on Twitter will give you 'influencer' status. If you share consistently great content, people will begin to avidly follow your tweets and add you to their lists.

# HOW DO I MEASURE MY SUCCESS?

## Focus on your target market!

If you haven't already thought about your particular market, see the Define Your Customer Profile and answer the questions about who your customers are, so that you can build up customer profiles and begin to research content that will make them smile, click or share your content and links.

Write a list of topics that complement your products and will interest your Twitter followers. You can use this list as a starting point to find Twitter users who may be interested in your brand and begin to build lists of users who share relevant content.

It's important that you remember the goal of your activity on Twitter as on other networks.

You need to set targets for growth month by month. Your time is precious and it's vital to know if your activity online is having a positive effect. Note that not all of the effects of your tweeting can be measured purely from direct clicks that lead to sales. The positive feeling that a customer has towards your brand after reading your updates, even if they choose not to click a link, comment or share online, cannot be measured directly.

Like all social networks, Twitter is what you make of it. The more active you are, the better the experience will be and the more interest you will create. As with all online networking, the content of your posts and the quality of your interactions are what will ultimately bring you traffic and followers, and hopefully a great return on your investment of time!

## GENERAL KEY PERFORMANCE INDICATORS (KPIS) FOR TWITTER

» Number of new followers / percentage follower growth
» Retweets
» Mentions
» Favourites
» Number of lists you are added to
» Clicks through to your website
» Leads generated (these could be both promotional leads and sales leads)

> *Having thousands of followers on Twitter can give your brand gravitas, but it doesn't necessarily equate to traffic and sales. You still have to share interesting and engaging content.*

## Twitter advertising

Just as with Facebook, you can promote tweets or your account in order to 'buy' follows or retweets. The Twitter advertising area is simple to use with lots of help to understand how your money will be spent. Find out at: https://ads.twitter.com.

As with all advertising, you need to be very clear about your goals and the return on investment that you expect for an advert to be considered successful. For example, it could be beneficial to promote a Tweet with details of a competition that you want to get shared in order to bring more traffic to your site, or you could just promote your account to instantly find followers without having to spend time searching for them.

Having thousands of followers on Twitter can give your brand gravitas, but it doesn't necessarily equate to traffic and sales. You still have to share interesting and engaging content.

# GOOGLE +

Don't underestimate the value of Google+ to your networking, especially the array of Google communities. Google+ has a great deal to offer and it is growing in popularity, partly owing to the way Google has positioned it as an integral part of many of its products, such as YouTube, Blogger, Picasa and Gmail.

> **MAGGY WOODLEY, RED TED ART**
>
> Google+ has been a great platform to explore and experiment with. It is a kind of mixture of Pinterest and Facebook - without the restrictions that Facebook puts on pages and with the added benefits of providing some SEO juice.

> Don't underestimate the value of Google+ to your networking, especially the array of Google communities.

## How can a Google+ account help grow your business?

Just as with any other social media network, Google+ offers you the chance to connect with new people and to reinforce existing connections. Google is continually updating and tweaking its algorithm to provide the very best search results to search queries. The more you share with Google+ the better, as you can directly connect your website and your 'authorship' of a website from your personal Google+ account.

Google has taken all of the amazing benefits that the Twitter Lists offer and created an entire network around it, just changing lists to 'circles'. As someone who loves to cut out the noise of social networks and focus on networking, I think this is fantastic. Instead of having Circles as an option, like Twitter Lists, it actively encourages you to add people to circles.

You want the biggest search engine in the world to be constantly updated about your craft business, don't you?

# "You want the biggest search engine in the world to be constantly updated about your craft business, don't you"

## Setting up a Google+ Page

Create a Google+ Profile (https://plus.google.com) and then create a Google+ Business page for your brand. You will also need a Google account to set up your Google Analytics in order to track your website and blog traffic.

Ensure that you complete all of the sections in full, especially where you need to add links to your websites and network profiles.

Once you have set up your Google+ profile at https://plus.google.com/u/0/pages/create, this link will take you to the 'create page' area or you can click on the 'house' symbol in the left hand column of quick links.

You will be taken through the page creation process step by step. Look at the 'Creating Powerful Profiles Pages' section to ensure you optimize your profile for search and follows!

## Google+ basics

### Circles

Unlike Facebook, Google does not currently use an algorithm to determine what you see in your Google+ news feed. Instead, it relies on you deciding which groups of people you are following. This is another good reason to have a Google+ account. It gives you a different experience from Facebook and allows you to see content you have requested to see.

These groups are known as circles. Many people get confused by the idea of circles, but it's just a word for groups of people. It is similar to adding people to a Twitter List, except Google+ expects you to add people to circles, whereas Twitter seems to hide its fantastic list feature away.

You can add any person or business to a circle. You can view all updates or click to see just the 'feeds' of updates from particular circles. How you curate your circles is entirely up to you!

## Google Hangouts

Google Hangouts is an instant messaging and video chat platform and is a very popular feature for networking and building your profile. Using 'Google Hangouts on air' (as opposed to private hangouts) your video conferences can be broadcast live on Google+ and be recorded. These videos also become part of your YouTube channel's offering. This can be a great way of showing that you are an influencer within your online community, whether you create your own mini-conferences or join others. Google's Help pages have all the details for starting and joining a hangout. If you are hosting a hangout, it is important to prepare topics and questions in advance to ensure the conversation flows well and that the resulting video becomes a useful resource for your followers.

## GOAL GROUPS

I advise splitting circles into goal groups – particular types of people you want to connect with, such as Top Bloggers, Complementary Bloggers, Suppliers, Industry Experts – you can, of course, be a little more creative with the names. Use my advice on creating Twitter Lists earlier in this chapter and be sure you follow up and actively interact with your groups, otherwise the administration time spent finding people to connect with will be wasted.

*Stop and think before posting a link. Make sure it's interesting!*

POST

**?** "Is your content angled to engage with your followers"

### Sharing circles

You can share circles with people, but the name of the list will not be shared. Your circles are private to you. Of course, Google will always be interested in the circles you create for advertising purposes and 'suggest ' people and brands/businesses to others to follow.

When writing a post, you can choose for the post to be public or to share it with a specific circle alone. When you post on Google+ you are given this option at the end of the post.

### Post content

Add in lots of relevant keywords to your page and follow the same principles of engaging users as discussed for Facebook networking earlier in this chapter. Stop and think before posting a link. Make sure it's interesting! Mix up relevant content and links and add in lots of great photos.

Using an asterix before and after a word or sentence will make that section appear in bold text – useful for adding emphasis to words and also creating headings for your Google+ posts.

# The test of a good post

» Is it angled to engage with your followers?

» People want to chat – could you ask a question?

» Can you share an interesting anecdote?

» Is your post chatty rather than sales orientated?

### Networking on Google+

The +1 on Google is equivalent to a like on Facebook. When someone clicks +1 on your posts, it will have an impact on your ranking in searches. This is because Google tailors results based on people's connections and location, and will incorporate results as recommendations.

Encouraging people to +1 your website or blog means that when their Google+ friends do a search, your page could come up near the top with a +1 from them – a personal recommendation and an incentive to click. This is similar to the way Facebook shows who likes a page from your friends when you see a Facebook widget on a website, except people see these recommendations not just when they arrive at a site but while they are searching.

Just as with Facebook and Pinterest, be sure to comment on posts and reply to comments on your own posts. You will see all notifications and it's worth checking in as often as possible to continue a conversation and develop connections.

### Google+ Communities

Google+ has communities, very similar to Facebook Groups and LinkedIn Groups. You can create a post on your page and choose to share it directly within the discussion areas of the groups. Google has seen how effective this has been with LinkedIn and has chosen to use this feature. Unfortunately, you cannot share a post to multiple groups at the same time. In my opinion, sharing posts on a group by group basis rather than sharing to multiple groups at the same time, is more time consuming but leads to more engaged communities as people make more effort.

Join as many relevant Google+ communities as you can find, and add a reminder to your schedule to post an update. Engage with the group members by sharing and +1-ing their posts and you will be rewarded with new contacts and loyal followers.

# YOUTUBE

YouTube is owned by Google, and once you create your Google+ account you can add a YouTube account and create a YouTube Channel which people can subscribe to. As with all social media channels, subscribers will see your latest video posts in a news feed from all the channels to which they subscribe.

All you need to create tutorials and video posts is a smartphone, PC or laptop with a webcam. You can also create a YouTube channel purely to curate other people's videos so don't immediately dismiss YouTube as a social network if you are a little camera shy.

## How is YouTube useful for your craft business?

Videos are incredibly useful for people who want to see your product in real life. You can use YouTube videos as a way of fully exploring the features and benefits of your products. You can treat your YouTube videos as an extension of your blogging. Instead of writing about it, make a video!

It may seem counterproductive to explain to people how to make your products – and it is! Instead you need to think of quick tutorials or posts that are engaging to watch and provide answers to people searching for information. Just as you do when researching a blog post, think about what your target audience wants to find out, not just about your products but in general. Could you regularly post a two to five-minute video that would be of interest to these people?

Video bloggers, or vloggers, can be amazingly successful. If you are happy to be on screen, I recommend that you share videos, which can support all of your online activity.

Increased traffic and subscribers will come if you can post 'how to' tutorials with tips on how to make an item or overcome a problem. More than ever before, people search YouTube directly for information and by providing them with the know-how in a video tutorial, you will win subscribers.

*Instead of writing about it, make a video!*

PLAY

VIDEO ▶

# YouTube Basics

» **Setting up**
YouTube has a huge help section for businesses and channel owners: www.YouTube.com/yt/playbook/channel-optimization.html

When you set up your channel, create a welcome video for newcomers in which you briefly explain what your channel is all about.

» **Editing videos and adding links**
You can use YouTube's own video-editing software to perfect your videos if you don't have access to other more sophisticated video editing software.

Add annotations to your video, which allow you to add clickable text in the video to subscribe to your channel or your Google+ account. All of the features for managing and editing videos, including adding these important links, can be found in the Video Manager area of YouTube.

» **YouTube sections and playlists**
YouTube allows you to create sections and playlists where you can create different groups of videos and neatly curate videos, so that people looking at your channel can quickly find the videos they want to watch. It can seem overwhelming to set this up, but as you add videos of your own and from others that suit your audience, you will see your channel taking shape and be able to better curate the sections. Soon you will be able to create a rich channel that will engage your target audience and lead to increased subscribers.

## Getting your videos watched!

Use the advice I have shared on SEO (see 'The essentials of content marketing') to ensure that every video you create has the right title and description to show up in a search. You should also include clickable links by ensuring links include the full http:// start. A video with 100,000 views but no link to find out more is a waste!

You can regularly promote your videos through all of your other social media accounts. Videos are content just like any blog post, so you can either promote them directly or embed them into a blog post. It's easy to embed a video by clicking on the 'sharing' settings beneath any YouTube video and clicking on 'embed'. You will then be given a snippet of code to add to your blog post or website.

Having an introductory video on your website can be a great way of catching people's attention and getting them to stay longer on your site, especially if coupled with 'in video' annotations where a viewer can click text in the video to subscribe to your channel.

Tweeting someone or sharing a link on a company's Facebook page to a video you think they'll find interesting or useful can be far more effective than simply sharing an image.

### Videos of products

Share videos that support your product listings and descriptions. You can link to or embed these videos in blog posts. These videos will emphasize the benefits and features of your products. For example, you could show how a bag you have made unzips easily and how beautiful the lining is – this may be difficult to achieve through photographs alone. There are so many ways that a video can highlight the features of your product more than a photo can, especially when the voice of the maker is there to take the viewer through all of the features.

### Videos of Works in Progress (#wips)

Take a video that shows the way your product is constructed. Showing the time and effort that goes into a piece and the artist at work is a great way of adding value to a finished product. It also shows off your unique skill and voice. Practise by positioning the camera or phone at a prime viewing angle while you work. You can use simple editing tools to cut snippets of video together and also include images. Try a programme such as Windows Movie Maker or use YouTube's own editing software.

### Blog posts vs vlog posts

If you feel confident in front of a camera, then make your next blog post a vlog (video blog) instead. People love to hear your voice and it's straightforward to embed a video post into your blog. Click 'embed' in the share settings and copy and paste the code snippet created into a blog post.

You will benefit from the views from your existing readership and also from people searching on YouTube. Videos are shown in Google's search results and can bring people directly to your video posts.

# BUILDING SUBSCRIBERS

» As with all your social networks, link to your account on your website or blog to ensure people notice that you have a YouTube presence.

» Regularly posting videos with optimized titles and descriptions is the best way to build your subscriber numbers organically in the right market.

» Use your contacts from other networks to bring interest to your YouTube channel.

» Just as you can guest blog for someone, you could also guest vlog.

» Invite people to appear on your channel as special guests, perhaps offering a tutorial for an item that complements your own products. You can do all of this via email, Skype and Google+ hangouts – you don't need to meet up in person to collaborate!

*Using videos to help people quickly understand your brand*

I regularly receive emails and tweets from companies asking me to promote their products with a post or share their videos. The companies that send me a quick one- or two-minute YouTube video really catch my attention – no one has the time to sit through ten minutes!

This video could be about a specific product you make or an overview of your designs. Be sure that the video is highly relevant to the people you share it with. For example, if you are reaching out to fashion bloggers, it needs to have a fashion-led angle, showing that your product looks fantastic, meets the current trends and is desirable.

## MAGGY WOODLEY, RED TED ART

My favourite feature of Google+ is its hangouts. They are a great way to connect with fellow bloggers, share information and create content for YouTube!

*Keep videos short – no one has the time to sit through ten minutes!*

## Video budget

Your videos need to look good – that's not to say they have to be ultra slick, just not so amateur that they devalue your products. With camera phones, you can take great-looking videos yourself but you may want to take videos with your products out and about, showing them off outside of your craft studio.

I've appeared in videos for clients and worked with professional video makers. They know exactly what they need in terms of footage to make a film, whereas amateurs often fail and waste time, or don't get the best shot. Paying a professional video maker is costly though. My advice is to approach local colleges where there may be photography and videography students willing to create videos for a reduced fee or even for free as work experience. You could also look into online courses to improve your video-making skills.

# INSTAGRAM

Instagram is a social networking channel that allows you to share updates via videos and images taken on your mobile phone.

## How is Instagram useful for your craft business?

Instagram is a wonderful site for adding interest to your brand and building awareness. Your posts can have a huge reach if they are relevant to your target market and hashtagged correctly, bringing influential people and potential customers over to you.

Each user has a home area where they see a chronological stream of posts from people and businesses they have chosen to follow. They can also search by hashtags, finding new and interesting images and instagrammers to follow.

Instagram is owned by Facebook. When you share a picture or like a picture on Facebook you can use it to create a Facebook post. Facebook has an interest in bringing Instagrammers together on Facebook so it will naturally give your Instagram posts a higher 'affinity' score with people who also use Instagram.

As a craft business owner you have the upper hand on Instagram – you are right next to all of the work you create and you can use it to tell a story about your business, taking amazing pictures of the details of your craft space, your work and inspiration.

Instagram has a success for business blog: http://business.instagram/blog/ It has some really useful and interesting articles and often features success stories from brands with tips on how they have engaged their target market through their images and hashtags.

> ### SARAH CORBETT, CRAFTIVIST COLLECTIVE
>
> Instagram is my favourite social media channel. I'm a visual person so I love looking at other people's images as well as sharing images of our projects and what we love. I prefer Instagram to Pinterest personally and I'm much more confident sharing images than words.

Instagram is a visual network. People take pictures with their camera phones and share them with their followers. As on all the networks, you can add hashtags to unite communities with a common theme, tag people and add comments on each other's posts.

> Use Instagram to tell a story about your business, taking amazing pictures of your craft space, work and inspiration.

# Tips for successful Instagramming!

» **Take sharp pictures with your phone**
Practise, practise, practise – there really is no other way to ensure that when the time comes you know exactly how to take a good picture. Look through all the settings your smartphone offers for close-up, day- and night-time images.

» **Develop your Instagram style**
Instagram offers various filters that subtly change and improve the photo by adding warmth or high contrast. You don't need to use the same filter each time, but it's great to see an Instagram account that has a theme that runs through all of its images – a visual style.

This theme could be 'fun', by looking at objects from an unusual angle, or you could chart your daily activity as an artist – the ups and downs of your working day. You don't have to be an amazing photographer to create beautiful collections of Instagram images.

Think about what your target market might enjoy apart from your craft. If you have an allotment or vegetable plot they may be fascinated to see your progress. Even a daily dog walk can provide people with a snapshot of life from your perspective.

» **Take more pictures!**
You can Instagram a picture right now or later but if you don't have the picture you can't Instagram! Taking pictures of all sorts of aspects of you and your business is crucial for Instagram success, and also gives you lots

> *Fun videos that capture a little snapshot of your world will add interest to blog posts.*

of opportunities for blog posts too. Never be without your phone! Instagram itself suggests that businesses need to 'find beauty everywhere'. If you work with beautiful fabrics or yarns, this is not difficult.

» **Embed Instagram pictures in your blog posts**
Click on 'share' on an Instagram picture and you are given the option to embed a post. This is a great way to let blog readers know you are an Instagrammer and help cross-promote your account, boosting follower numbers. If you have successful blog posts that bring in traffic using keywords that fit your brand, you could embed an Instagram picture in order to give new visitors to your site the opportunity to connect with you on this very popular platform.

» **Short videos**
Instagram allows you to take 15-second videos – you can use this feature to show yourself at work. If you find you are good at making little videos, you may want to look into joining www.vine.com, a network purely for sharing videos. Brands are having similar success on Vine as they are on Instagram. You can't add hyperlinks on Vine and Instagram so they are not useful for getting clicks, but they are great for raising brand awareness.

Keep an eye on how long it takes you to set up a mini video and whether it adds any value to your brand. Videos that are poor quality could have a negative effect. Fun videos that capture a little snapshot of your world will add interest to blog posts.

> ## LAUREN O'FARRELL, KNIT THE CITY
>
> Vine is my tip for adding an essential skill to your social media kung fu. Easy peasy to film stop-motion craft that will hook followers in six seconds.

## Who is following you?

Keep up to date with who follows you on Instagram. You will be notified of new followers – check your settings area to edit these notifications. Be sure to follow them back if you like what you see and take time to comment on any relevant posts.

Take a look at a new follower's bio and reinforce the connection by posting a tweet or Facebook message. These little extra touches when networking can make the difference between a one-time follow and lots of interaction.

People who follow you on Instagram give you an excuse to take a conversation to the next level beyond Instagram and social networking. If they have a website, you could send an email saying thanks for the follow, and ask if they would be interested in featuring your work.

## Networking on Instagram

Many people use Instagram more than they use Facebook, Twitter and Pinterest. As the success of Facebook wanes, especially in the younger market, networks such as Instagram, Snapchat and Vine are set to see further growth and more opportunities for businesses to advertise and network 'creatively'.

Be sure to add comments and like others' posts, not just on followers' pages but by searching for relevant hashtags and recent updates within your niche topics. Without networking or adding relevant hashtags, your Instagram profile will be invisible to those outside your immediate following.

Look at the likes, comments and hashtags of people you consider to be influencers and check them regularly so you can follow and network with relevant Instagrammers and become part of a group. Remember to look out for opportunities where you can invite Instagrammers to post on your blog or ask if they ever accept guest blogs.

If there is an influential blogger that you have connected with via Facebook, Twitter, Google+ or Pinterest, then ensure they know that you are also on Instagram.

> ## FORGET ABOUT SELLING
>
> Posting images of work for sale with a price in the comments is considered spammy on Instagram. You can still post images of finished pieces, but be more creative about how you include the piece. It could be next to a sewing machine and a large slice of cake with the comment, 'I deserve this, the pockets on this bag take serious concentration #cake #etsy #fashion'

## AMANDA CUSICK, KITSCHYCOO

Instagram has been the newest social media platform that I just adore, and I think it's really changing the nature of blogging. I heard a lot of people saying that they're considering scaling down or even stopping blogging in lieu of Instagram because sharing is so much easier, faster and more engaging.

## TAGGING TIPS

» When you share a post as a fun idea, you can ask people to tag someone – for example, 'Tag a friend who deserves these chocolates' (alongside a relevant image of delicious-looking chocolates).

» You may get a reply '@hilaryhaptree deserves a chocolate because she has just helped me understand the purpose of Instagram tagging!'

» I would then see the post and could thank that person for tagging me and also add to the post by tagging someone else. I could follow the person who sent me the comment.

» Be sure your tags have relevance. If you tag people too much they will feel it is harassment and report you as a spammer.

### Tag people

You can tag people in your caption and in the comments of other people's posts. It's the same method as with Twitter, Facebook and Pinterest. You just need to type @name – the user's name then becomes a link to their profile and they get a notification that you have mentioned them.

### Update regularly!

Update regularly but only when you have something good to share. You need to hunt out images and let your creative mind find interest in even the most mundane. If you have taken lots of pictures on one day, then spread out these images across a day or week. You can give them a collective hashtag to show they are part of a series of images.

Over posting – that is, lots of posts in quick succession – is regarded as bad etiquette on Instagram.

### Regrams

Instagram doesn't offer a share feature at the moment. There are apps available for reposting others' content or RG #regram, or regramming, as you will see it called. New apps and features for social media arrive all the time, so it's best to search for the latest. I use the apps Repost and Statigram, which both allow you to repost and share content.

Only regram posts you think are amazing and always tag the original Instagram poster in the comments. This is to thank them and also a way of connecting with influencers and showing your appreciation for their work. Be sure to use the tag #RG or #regram so your followers are aware it is not your original content.

### Optimize old posts

You can add hashtags into the comments of your posts to enable them to come up in the search results for more and more searches within your niche market.

For example, on a photograph of a slice of cake you may have originally posted #cake #baking. However, in the comments you can add #nomnomnom #chocolateaddict #chocaholic #GBBO and more to ensure your post gets seen by more people. As you discover new hashtags you can add these too, ensuring you make the most of older posts.

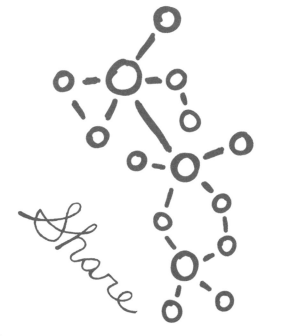

### Share settings

Currently on Instagram you can autoshare to one Facebook stream (choose between your page or your personal profile), Twitter, Flickr, Tumblr and more.

While you can instantly share your Instagram posts across many channels at once, you can also share your posts to these networks later. This will allow you to stretch the life of an image across the day. This can be especially useful if you are Instagramming a live event but you don't want to bombard Facebook with images.

You can also take pictures with your phone wherever you are and look through your images later, choosing just to share the best of them once you have time to edit them and think of good captions. This is far better than sending out a stream of posts all at once to your social media channels.

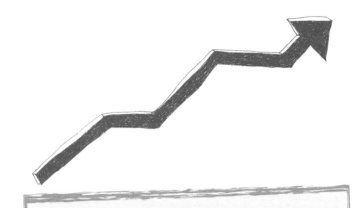

## MEASURING INSTAGRAM SUCCESS

There are third-party apps and websites available that will analyse the resonance of your hashtags and posts on Instagram. However, when your account is brand new and still fairly small it's usually very obvious if you are reaching out to the right people or if your posts are falling flat.

The success of a post and an Instagram account can be measured by likes, comments and follows. Keep an eye on hashtags that work well to bring you new likes and followers. You may find that embedding Instagram images in your blog posts will bring you many more likes – capitalize on this and look at old posts where you can add relevant Instagrams or Instagram videos.

As with the other social channels, in the early days you cannot expect one social channel to drive masses of traffic to your website. Instead, focus on who to network with and how you can develop relationships with influencers and bloggers on Instagram.

### Inspire others

Your photos need to make people think. You want your followers to think, 'I like that, I want that, I want to be there'. They will enjoy your posts if they feel they have a connection. Inspire them by posting beautiful, funny, interesting and exciting pictures. If you are halfway through a project, think about how you can photograph it best to make people understand your skill, and the time, effort and joy you have in making it.

### Be inspired!

Instagram, like all social networks, is full of inspiration. In particular, you can use other people's Instagram posts to create wonderful themed posts.

## Instagram advertising

Instagram is currently just using advertising for selected partners in order to test the waters for what works. It is keen to keep users on side and not flood them with adverts without knowing exactly how they will respond. Keep an eye on the Instagram blog for details.

> You can use other people's Instagram posts to create wonderful themed posts.

# LINKEDIN

LinkedIn is a fantastic platform for networking and I believe that everybody with a business or service to offer should set up a profile on LinkedIn. Even if you find you are too busy with the rest of your social marketing campaign to use LinkedIn for networking you should definitely make time to create a free profile.

LinkedIn is used by businesses and individuals across all industries but its popularity within the creative industry is growing rapidly. Through creating connections (like friends and followers on Twitter and Facebook) you can network and keep up to date with the latest craft industry news. Your Linkedin profile works as an online CV and can be a great place to flex your muscles as an expert in your particular area.

For example, if a magazine editor needed to commission a fabric designer for a feature, they would search for 'Fabric Designer' and a list of results will come up which could then be filtered by region and connections. In business it's always good to get a reference, and each connection you make on LinkedIn is like a mini referral.

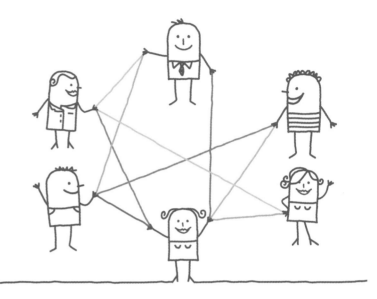

## PATRICIA VAN DER AKKER, THE DESIGN TRUST

I find LinkedIn incredibly useful for market research. I know that many creatives find it a little boring, but if you are looking for the names of buyers, for example, then it is really useful. Also, if you want to get any referrals (one of the best marketing techniques, especially if you provide services) then you can type in the name of the person you want to contact and see if any of your contacts know them. This works particularly well if you have a good selection of contacts already. You can then ask your existing connection to do an intro email for you, which will often ensure that doors will open for you.

## Creating a powerful profile on LinkedIn

Treat completing your LinkedIn profile as seriously as you would if applying for a job. This isn't to say you can't be selective about your experience and leave out jobs and experience that aren't relevant, but it does need to be professional. Take your time to gather as much information as possible about you and your craft business.

# Setting up your profile

» Go to LinkedIn to set up your profile. LinkedIn will lead you through setting up your profile step by step.

» Use keywords in the summary (bio/description) and make sure these keyword phrases can be found in your previous work experience and in the projects areas.

» Write a list of your skills and focus on what someone may be searching for when they are looking for your skills and expertise.

» Include details of specific projects and publications in the relevant sections to add extra interest to your profile.

» LinkedIn has an excellent help centre and a forum where you can ask any technical questions: http://help.linkedin.com/app/home

## RECOMMENDATIONS

Ask people you know well or customers you have found are already on LinkedIn for a recommendation – these are powerful additions and add enormous credibility to your profile. The more recommendations you have the better. If you write good recommendations for other people, it can be a good ice breaker to ask them to reciprocate, but it shouldn't be expected. You want the recommendations to be genuine and well written.

Also use the 'endorse' feature to let people know you appreciate their expertise and skills. LinkedIn will give you the opportunity to endorse your connections when you sign in, so if someone deserves your endorsement, don't be shy about clicking.

## Using LinkedIn

Not just for stuffy business people or head hunters, LinkedIn can be used when you want to quickly share your experience and expertise with a new contact.

For example, if your Twitter networking has paid off and you have acquired the email of an editor of a magazine or blog, you can send a brief email about your latest product line or the article/blog post you would like to write for them, and simply add a line at the end of the email directing them to your profile: 'Please take a look at my LinkedIn profile for further details of my experience.'

It's a great opportunity to 'connect' on another level with these influential people. Once you have someone's email address you can invite them to become a contact. The more of these influential 'connections' you have, the better your profile will appear. The more often it will be viewed and the greater the chance you will be discovered by potentially influential people.

You can also add your LinkedIn profile to your email signature so if the reader wants to quickly find out who you are, they can find all of your links and experience in one place.

## LinkedIn as a social network

The same basic principles of networking apply to LinkedIn. Your interactions on LinkedIn are shared in an activity stream and you can create useful connections.

However, LinkedIn is much more professional than other social networks and geared towards making business-to-business connections, and learning and developing businesses through the many groups that are available.

You can share updates on your company, links to your latest blog posts and you can like and comment on posts exactly as on Facebook. However, it is definitely not the place to try any direct selling because you won't be connecting with individual customers here.

On LinkedIn you can share exciting product news, such as 'I've designed a new range' or 'We're exhibiting at ...'. This is more appropriate than saying, 'I've listed this in my shop'. Use Facebook, Twitter and Google+ for your more chatty posts, and share any useful industry news you discover on your other social networks on your LinkedIn account to encourage discussion among your industry connections.

## Following up off and online events and meetings

If you meet a useful contact on or offline and you aren't already connected on LinkedIn, use LinkedIn as a way of strengthening that relationship. Invite them to connect and add a personal message, such as 'Hi, we met at the show yesterday. I loved your watermelon fabric – would be great to continue our chat about an interview for my blog.'

The person you met will then be able to see your 'CV' and be reminded about your great work with their fabrics. They may be keen to feature your work on their own website. If they add you as a contact, be sure to interact with them and keep the relationship 'hot' until you have reached the desired goal of a link back to your site or some mutual promotion.

It's all about building on little interactions that lead to bigger and better connections and getting your name and your work out there so people find you online through searches. When someone asks them, 'Do you know anyone who…?', you hope they will reply, 'Yes, I know just the person on LinkedIn – I'll introduce you!' This has happened to me on a number of occasions and has led to business from new clients.

## A WORD OF WARNING

LinkedIn wants its members to have genuine professional connections. In the early days of your account it will be fairly lenient about who you connect with but you will be penalized by the site if you contact too many people you do not know. People can reply to a connection with 'I don't know this person' and that can leave you labelled as a spammer if it happens too many times.

## Connect with more people

» Add everyone on your existing business email lists – there is a simple 'Import Contacts' tool: www.linkedin.com/fetch/importAndInvite

» Invite contacts through LinkedIn's 'people you may know' suggestions, another useful way to quickly add people to your contacts: www.linkedin.com/people/pymk

» Invite people who have given you their business cards at events, fairs and shows. You will be asked to add their email address as a way of proving that you have a genuine connection.

» Remind people where you met them in your message, for example, you may have met them on Twitter and have acquired their email address from their website. You might write, 'Hi, we're following each other on Twitter – I'm @haptree – would be great to connect on LinkedIn too.'

» Tell people you are on LinkedIn. Set up a scheduled regular Tweet or Facebook post to go out that says, 'Are you on LinkedIn? I'm www.linkedin.com/in/haptree – would be great to connect, so please add me as a connection.'

## Groups

As with Google+ and Facebook, you can join as many relevant groups as you want. Your posts and replies will be seen by niche groups of people who will begin to see you as an 'influencer' on your particular topic and not just on LinkedIn.

Join in discussions and start your own but do not use groups to create links to your products or try to promote sales. Share your group discussions on Facebook or Twitter to further their reach.

Add discussion sharing to your social media weekly schedule. It will prompt you to network on LinkedIn at the same time and provide great content for your other networks. Write a list of the groups and communities you have joined on various social networks not just LinkedIn. You can then make a quick decision about which groups suit your latest post and/or any posts you wrote before you discovered those groups.

You can also consider writing a blog post specifically with a LinkedIn community in mind. The beauty of communities (and groups on all social networks) is that they are full of questions that you can try to answer and establish yourself as an authority.

## Sharing on other networks

Always think about how you can halve the time used and double your exposure by sharing content with more than one network or community. For example, you could use Twitter to try and boost responses to your latest LinkedIn discussion:

'@usefulcontact I wondered if you had any thoughts on this discussion http://linkedin.com/xyz

That's intelligent engagement marketing at its best! Your contact may be keen to get involved and will reply either on Twitter or to the LinkedIn discussion itself. This technique of sharing discussions and actively sharing with specific industry influencers works well with Facebook posts and discussions in Google+ groups too.

## Measuring your success on Linkedin

Linkedin is one of the tools you can use to strengthen relationships as part of your overall online marketing strategy to connect with influencers. Your success on Linkedin should largely be measured by how fruitful your networking is and how many new leads you can generate. You may see some traffic to blog posts you add on the site but this is not your primary focus with Linkedin. Far more important is the networking aspect.

### CRAIG DE SOUZA, CRAFT & HOBBY ASSOCIATION

Securing a meeting, especially with some of the bigger buyers, can be difficult. Use every method you can think of to establish you presence. LinkedIn groups are really good for getting noticed, and becoming involved in groups and conversations. You need your target buyer to recognize your offering so that when you approach them they recognize your company. Don't rely on just one method. It takes time to be seen and be noticed, but the more you do the more chance you have of achieving success.

# REMEMBER YOUR ABCs

This is the important checklist I discussed in 'Is social networking worth your time and energy?' that you need to think about when sharing any content. Remember 'Acquisition, Behaviour and Conversion' – your social media strategy needs the ABC approach. Let's recap now we have looked at the biggest social media channels you can use in your online marketing campaign.

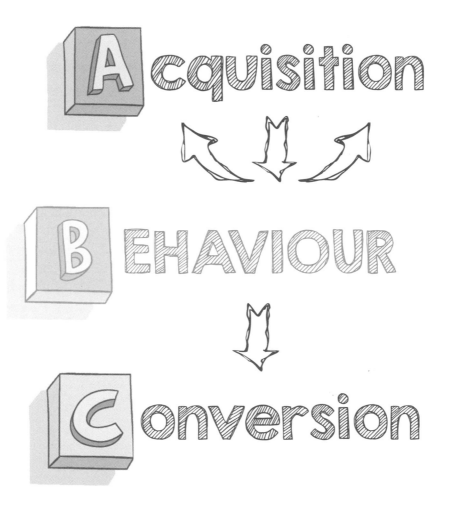

## Acquisition – getting people to your website

Your social media strategy should be designed to draw existing fans and new people to your website and social media channels through sharing links to interesting content and beautiful, clickable images.

Engage people with questions and your posts will stop being merely broadcasts. People who are engaged with your posts are more likely to interact with future posts. Create a variety of social media posts that are designed to build awareness, such as sharing a humorous or inspiring image and other posts that link back to your website.

The acquisition process can take time. Someone who finds you on social media and follows or fans one of your accounts will not automatically visit your website unless you work out in your strategy a good reason why they should. Getting that first engagement, whether it is a like, follow, comment or share, is the start. Regularly sharing information they need or will enjoy is the next step.

## Behaviour – what people do on your website

Ensure that the posts you are sharing on your website have links to allow people to further explore your site and connect with all of your channels by including social icons. Allowing people to just bounce away once they have read a post is a mistake many people make when blogging and promoting their blog posts on social media, they forget this important next step and don't optimize the posts they are working hard to build traffic to. Clicks mean nothing if that's all they are.

Keeping people on your site for longer and viewing lots of pages is important to help make Google and other search engines see that your content is engaging. However, make sure you also have clear calls to action to share your content; each click is potentially someone new marketing your work to their network.

There are many widgets, plugins and gadgets you can add to your site to enable people to share content with just one click. Try installing www.addthis.com on your blog or website. I have used it for years with great results.

> Clicks through from your social media networking and posting mean nothing unless you optimize a post to convert the traffic.

## Conversion – getting customers

Have you added links to your products within your posts? If your latest blog post is being promoted by you and retweeted on Twitter or pinned on Pinterest, you want to ensure it has at least one mention of a product within it and isn't purely an interesting article about gardening or fashion.

Create a relevant post that attracts people who may be interested in looking at your products or, as a micro conversion, signing up to your newsletter. Your goal should be to convert clicks into subscribers or customers. Without adding links, social media icons, social sharing options and reminders to sign up in the sidebars of your blog or website, or within the actual blog post, people will read your post and leave. Clicks through from your social media networking and posting mean nothing unless you optimize a post to convert the traffic.

Creating a cross-channel content strategy

Here's where I get more specific about how you can use all of the networks to their best advantage, ensuring that you maximize the efficiency of each piece of content, whether it's a single image or an entire blog post, curated content or your own work.

# BUILDING YOUR ONLINE MARKETING STRATEGY

As we have just recapped, you need to remember the **ABC** of your online marketing strategy – **Acquisition** (getting people involved), **Behaviour** (getting them to interact, click around your site and talk about your craft business) and **Conversion** (getting them to subscribe or buy).

You should have this cycle in mind every time you are online networking, researching and creating content to share.

## Creating an editorial calendar

Planning post themes in advance will save you time. Create a spreadsheet or use an online calendar service to give you an overview of the themes you want to address in your content strategy.

Your calendar does not need to be overly complex. Simply include dates, suggested themes, ideas for blog post titles for each month and keywords to use based on your research.

Set aside time each month to update your calendar and add in more detail to help focus your mind when researching and writing up your blog posts. Your editorial calendar should stretch at least six months ahead, just as you should be thinking well ahead to ensure you have time to market work at busy times of the year and to make and design your crafts.

Planning ahead also gives you the opportunity to send out timely emails to magazine editors and newspapers with news of designs, promotions and new ranges you are developing.

## TO CREATE A SUCCESSFUL STRATEGY YOU NEED TO DETERMINE THE FOLLOWING:

» Your target market – who are the relevant audience you want to engage with your brand?

» When are you going to update all the information feeds?

» What will you share?

» How much can be duplicated and reshared?

» Can any of your social profiles be automated to save time?

» How much time do you have to spend on networking each week?

» How much time should be devoted to researching suitable content?

STRATEGY!

## KIRSTY ELSON

I try to post something every day - usually in the evening - and this can act as a great incentive, as it spurs me on to finish a piece I may have started, so I have something new to show!

The following is an example calendar for a craft business where a designer is selling handmade bags, purses, fabric keyfobs and pdfs for patterns. I have given four blog-post examples, posting once a week – you may need to brainstorm more ideas depending on how much time you have. You need to do keyword research for your posts to ensure you are creating content that will be discovered through search and you have great post titles. Think of ways that you can incorporate your products and promotions into your blog posts by trying to theme any competitions or offers with the content theme for that week or month.

I create an outline plan like this, then I like to add my content ideas directly to an online calendar. I add in ideas for social media posts that fit around the themes as and when I think of them in my weekly scheduling and planning sessions, ensuring I am always a few weeks ahead when possible in terms of writing. Focusing on blog content to start with will help build in structure to your content plan as you develop it and add more detail. Just look at all this content – three hours of planning could see your blog topped up with relevant content every week without you even scratching your head. You will know exactly what to research and which promotions to plan for. You can also easily see where you can add internal links to older content, planning themes that run throught the year.

# EXAMPLE OF SOCIAL MEDIA CALENDAR FOR A CRAFT BUSINESS

| | JANUARY | FEBRUARY | MARCH | APRIL | MAY | JUNE |
|---|---|---|---|---|---|---|
| **Important Dates** | | Valentine's Day | Mothers' Day | Easter | Bank Holidays | Fathers' Day |
| **Sales, Promotions and Offers** | January Sale – 10% off selected stock | Free key fob with every purchase over £25 | Vouchers for Mothers' Day gifts | Easter offer – reductions on slow stock | 10% off kids pdf patterns | Sign up to newsletter and receive a free pattern |
| **Content Themes** | Organization and Planning | Eco friendly | Spring fashion | Weddings | Kids | Summer holidays |
| **Post Ideas** | How to never lose your keys! | Last minute eco gifts for women – gift guide for Valentine's Day | Latest fashions emerging – which bags to team with them | Bridesmaid bags – what they should carry? | 20 fun craft ideas for kids | Beach wear – handmade sarongs (plus beach bag pdf) |
| | News – the new range from Haptree Bags | Eco friendly fabrics (highlight the fabric bags are made of) | How to carry a bag with style – photos of celebs | How to make a simple bag for your bridesmaids – video tutorial | Reusable lined kids' sandwich bag – video tutorial | Fathers' Day key fobs |
| | Top 10 items to always carry in your handbag | Eco shopping bags – why have a supermarket bag when you can make your own? | Featured bag – the Haptree handbag – perfect Mothers' Day gift | Where to source ethical wedding supplies | Kids holdall patterns feature | Travelling light: essentials to pack – the Haptree Holdall perfect weekend bag |
| | How to sew a simple foldable shopper – tutorial/video tutorial | Eco friendly clothes shops | Does buying the latest fashions mean you have to compromise ethics (love fashion, hate sweatshops)? | Fun ring cushion tutorial – make your ring cushion unique to fit your wedding theme | Great magazines for kids that don't come with cheap plastic toys | Teachers' gift ideas to make – pdf pencil-case pattern to download when sign up to newsletter – video tutorial |
| **Competitions** | Win a key fob | Source prize from complementary craft business – knitting pattern for boot cuffs? | Win a book – ask publishers of any new fashion/sewing books for review copy to give away | Win a holdall pattern (and see if fabric supplier is interested in giving away vouchers) | Win a reusable kids sandwich bag (the one made from the tutorial) | Win a Fathers' Day key fob |

*Creating a cross-channel content strategy*

| JULY | AUGUST | SEPTEMBER | OCTOBER | NOVEMBER | DECEMBER |
|---|---|---|---|---|---|
| Summer holidays | Summer holidays | New school term | Halloween | Bonfire Night | Christmas |
| Christmas in July – 10% off everything | Discount for early-bird commissions for Christmas gifts | | Flash sale Halloween to Bonfire night – 10% off all patterns | | 10% off everything, depending on sales volume |
| Learn to sew | Summer fun | Gifts | Kids | Parties | Christmas |
| Tips for downloading pdf patterns – video tutorial | How to make bandanas – video tips | Gift guide – gifts for men (manly key fobs included) | Christmas shopping with toddlers – top tips for parents | The perfect party bag for a little black dress | Gift guide – last-minute Christmas gifts |
| How to read a sewing pattern | Beach security – secret pockets in the Haptree beach bag | Gift guide – handmade accessories for women | Best sewing machines for making kids' Christmas presents | Top designer dress styles to flatter | Five simple recipes for Christmas treats to make with kids |
| Free patterns for simple dresses on the Internet | 10 alcohol free kids' cocktails | Gift guide – gifts for kids. Simple sewing kits for kids (including pdf key fob pattern) | How to sew spooky bunting – video | 10 cocktail recipes for your Christmas party | Make-up bag tutorial; last-minute gift idea – video tutorial |
| Sewing kids' PJ bottoms – simple tutorial | Inexpensive activities for keeping kids occupied | Gift guide – eco friendly gifts from handmade designers | Sewing Christmas stockings using fabric scraps | Mini backpack feature – retro 90s backpacks for nightclubs | Happy Christmas post |
| Speak to sewing-course instructors and work out promo – discount off courses | Win a key fob | Source prize from a complementary craft business – back to school moleskine? | Win a book – ask publishers of any new craft/kids' books for review copy to give away | Win a holdall pattern | No competition – review the business year and plan for next year |

## Updating your networks

### Weekly posting and research schedule

I use a weekly schedule like the one on the following pages for each of my clients to ensure I create a balance of posts, promotional posts, posts to inspire and posts with specific networking goals.

You can print out a spreadsheet like this and keep it beside you when you do your weekly scheduling and content research. It is especially useful if you prefer to update your social media profiles live because it will keep you on track each day. You should tweak and adapt a schedule like this as you begin to measure results.

> If you feel your creativity is being compromised by your marketing schedule, it is time to reprioritize your weekly tasks.

» **Don't panic**
Arghhhh! You may feel totally overwhelmed by now with how many networks there are to keep updated and active. The way to deal with this feeling of panic is through sticking to your tight schedule of activity and sticking like glue to your social media strategy.

» **Keep it real!**
If you cannot complete everything you want to within the allotted time, your strategy and schedule are unrealistic for your craft business. Becoming frustrated by constantly not managing to achieve all the tasks on your plan can be soul destroying and leave you feeling overwhelmed. If you ever feel like your creativity is being compromised by your marketing schedule, then it is time to reprioritize your weekly tasks.

» **Plan your time wisely**
Your schedule itself will take time to create but it is important to keep networks 'alive' and to have planned activity sessions, with time allocated for searching for content, scheduling updates and live networking across each week. When paired with an 'editorial calendar' and fixed goals, the time you spend on social networking will be much more efficient and as a result you will have time to spend working on the other important aspects of your business.

» **Take time off**
Just like any job, you need down time! You love your craft – it's the reason you started a business around it. But if you don't give yourself a total break from either marketing it or making it, you are likely to burn out. Learn to close the laptop and shut the craft room door; you have scheduled some great updates and you don't need to be online all night. It's easy to get addicted to the buzz of likes and tweets and begin to neglect the important tasks, such as writing and researching blog posts, in favour of the instant gratification of chatting away on Facebook or Twitter. Use a timer if you struggle to tear yourself away.

> *Give networks time to develop and measure your success against your specific business goals, not just against likes or follows.*

## Make guest blogging a high priority

Networking with influencers should be at the top of your list of marketing priorities – getting your work into the media spotlight, whether on a blog or in a magazine. Being featured on influential blogs can have a 'snowball' effect, resulting in many more offers of interviews, magazine commissions and of course more media exposure, which will hopefully lead to more sales.

Offering to write guest blog posts or creating tutorials for publications is great for search engine optimization because you are creating quality links back to your site. It is also helpful for increasing your credibility as an expert and will help you to find new niche audiences to share your work with. For this reason 'guest blogging' ticks all of the 'high priority' boxes for me.

However, you won't be given the opportunity to write posts if you don't actively network, and you won't find the right blogs if you don't spend time researching your market. You always need to think of the bigger picture when marketing online, which is why having very specific goals in mind is so important to enable you to prioritize your schedule. Rarely would I ever accept a guest post from someone who has emailed me out of the blue.

Good guest posts take time to prepare and they need to be high quality. Be sure when you are offering to write a post for a site that you give people realistic dates for sending the content and you understand what they want in terms of technical details, such as the word count and images, and also artistic details, such as the angle of the post. Letting people down will damage your reputation and you may not be asked again. I look after a number of blogs for clients and it's not worth my time if I have to chase people up repeatedly for additional copy or images.

Factor in time for writing guest posts into your weekly or monthly schedule, and also consider the time needed for promoting them. Using my weekly schedule as an example, I would just replace one of the blog posts on my own site with one for an influencer's site. Once the guest post goes live, you can also post a snippet of it to your blog, or perhaps embed the Facebook post or tweet from the blogger when they share it on their networks to encourage more people to visit it. So don't worry if it means you have less content for your own site because you will still have a post to promote.

### Identify key channels

Identify which channels will be your focus when planning your posting schedule – you may feel that Facebook offers your business a great way to connect directly with customers. Conversely, you may discover through market research that your niche market is not particularly interested in Facebook and focusing on engaging with 'influencers' through Twitter and LinkedIn is a better prospect. This entirely depends on your particular voice and the crafts you are marketing.

Give networks time to develop and measure your success against your specific business goals not just against clicks, likes or follows. Use your findings to adapt where you prioritize your time online.

## Outline plan

This looks like a lot of work. However, each networking task may only take 15 minutes, and sharing and scheduling content for your Facebook and Google+ pages can be done in one sitting in advance each week, or for every few days. When you create your own outline posting schedule, write down a list of tasks you need to do to keep on top of your networking and spread these tasks across the days you have most time. For this example I have assigned a task to each day. In your case, you may only have the weekends free and need to spread these tasks over two weeks instead. The important thing is to be realistic. Assigning a task to a particular day can help you get into a routine and stop getting distracted.

### FIONA PULLEN, THE SEWING DIRECTORY

Social media can be a huge time suck. It is best to try to schedule in set time for social media activities and not constantly keep it open in the background distracting you. Using programs like Hootsuite or Tweet Deck to preschedule your updates, or prescheduling direct on Facebook, make life a lot easier. You can put aside a block of time to schedule your updates for the next few days and then you are free to get on with other things.

## EXAMPLE OF A WEEKLY SCHEDULE

|  | BLOG AND NEWSLETTER CONTENT |
|---|---|
| Notes | Plan, research keywords, write and schedule posts in advance |
| Monday | Tutorial/Useful information post |
| Tuesday | |
| Wednesday | Work in Progress Post/product post/Company News |
| Thursday | |
| Friday | Send newsletter |
| Saturday | Feature Post (content which links to complementary bloggers/influencers on your networking lists) |
| Sunday | |

*Creating a cross-channel content strategy*

| FACEBOOK / GOOGLE+ | NETWORKING TASKS |
|---|---|
| Use Facebook/Google+ as a framework for your content research. Researching the content to share on these channels will provide you with lots of opportunities for networking | Check in to all accounts as often as possible to network and share content and reply to comments. |
| Promote latest blog post | Check Twitter Lists, retweet, schedule and save interesting content – any industry posts to LinkedIn |
| Feature blogger/designer, tag and mention on other channels | |
| Share latest popular pin on Pinterest | Pinterest – find new accounts to follow/new board to complement blog content research |
| Chatty status update / question | LinkedIn – find people to connect with and groups to join |
| Promote latest blog post | Twitter – find new accounts to follow, create/update twitter lists |
| Share interesting info about your craft business/invite to sign up to the newsletter /competition | Facebook – find new fan pages to like |
| Interesting article/shared content from Twitter List/Pinterest research | Instagram – Hashtag research, find new accounts to follow |
| Feature blogger/designer, tag and mention on other channels | |
| Share latest Instagram | Google+ – find new accounts to follow, communities to join |
| Chatty status update | |
| Promote latest blog post | Check Twitter Lists, retweet, schedule and save interesting content |
| Inspiring image | Check YouTube channels, share content to playlists |
| Share latest/interesting Pinterest board to follow | |

# WHAT TO SHARE ON YOUR SOCIAL NETWORKS

Once you have your profiles up and running, your editorial calendar fleshed out and a posting schedule set up, the next thing to consider is the actual content!

You need to define what will resonate with your specific target market and on which social network. It's all about engagement! But how and where do you find this perfect, engaging content? There are two sources: your own original content or curated content.

## Sharing original content

The content you create is vital, but it can be hard to have a finished product to share every day. Think broadly about what your audience may find interesting about you and your work. A question, a frustration or a triumph can be all that is needed to share with your audience and get them involved with your social networks.

### POLLY DOUGDALE, HANDMADE HORIZONS

You might have thousands of people visiting your site, but if they can't navigate your online shop, or your products are not shown off to their full potential, the visitors will disappear without a trace. In order to convert browsers into buyers, always ensure that your product photography, pricing and product descriptions are up to scratch.

## Ideas for original images and blog posts to share

» **Work in progress**
People love to see how a product is made and giving them a sneak peek at the process really helps to add value to your work.

» **Frustrations**
You could talk about issues you are having with your work, with the Post Office or even just those days when everything seems to be going pear-shaped! We all love to console and commiserate when things don't go according to plan. See the funny side and share it.

» **Your workspace**
People are naturally nosy and might like a behind-the-scenes look at where you work and your tools. Just take the photos carefully so that they don't include anything unsightly. You need to project the right image, but even if your workspace is a little chaotic people will enjoy it – creativity is messy!

» **Inspiration for new designs**
Let us see the world through your eyes. If you see an inspiring pattern or image, share a picture and tell people all about it and how it has inspired you.

» **Questions**
Are you thinking of a new design? Why not ask and get some feedback? You could share a sketch or some colourways for a new product or packaging.

» **Completed pieces of work**
Why not show people a piece before it is listed or uploaded to your shop and has a price tag? This is more social – it shows you are proud of what you have made and people can then ask you how they can buy it! You can also share details of work on commission and orders, letting people see you are busy and in demand.

# TELL PEOPLE YOUR STORY

People love to get to know an artist – it connects them with the finished products that they buy. With an item of craft, hours of thought, frustration, love and hard work go into every piece. Getting to know the artist makes all this work real and is why we differentiate crafts and works of art from mass-produced goods. Crafts and art are a natural talking point – unique pieces made by a unique person!

Take care not to be too personal though. You will naturally get to a point where you feel familiar with your audience and you know your boundaries. Just have a check now and again that you aren't sharing too much personal information.

These insights into your world can be shared as longer blog posts but also just as snapshots of you and your work via your social networks. Instagram is great for posting quick, good-looking pictures that can be shared easily with your other networks.

# CURATING CONTENT

Curated content simply means content that is not original but is curated by you. By consistently sharing the best and most interesting posts within your niche, your followers will identify you as an influencer within your industry.

## Your research team

Don't have a research team? Yes, you do! Think of the bloggers and the people you follow on all of your social networks as a research team, all happily sharing the best and brightest content out there with you. They are producing original content and searching the far corners of the Internet to find amazing content that is available every time you log in.

With your unique taste, you can curate a stream of updates across your social networks that incorporate the best from all of these sources, creating a following and expressing all of the values of your brand by offering your unique opinions when you share content with your followers and fans.

## RSS feeds

An RSS feed reader enables you to follow blog posts in a stream of updated posts all from the same place. Most blogs have an RSS Feed to enable people to easily get updates through a feed reader. Most feed readers also enable you to quickly share posts and pin the content to Pinterest without having to click to the blog itself.

Make collecting blogs your new hobby. It's been my hobby for a while now – I have thousands on my lists!

It's easy to discover great bloggers as you are researching for a blog post or looking through Pinterest or your social networks. The key is to file that blogger into your chosen RSS feed reader so that you can keep up with their latest posts and find further shareable content in the future.

There are many RSS Feed readers and news aggregator sites to choose from. My favourite is currently Bloglovin. com and I also like Feedly.com. I use Bloglovin alongside my Social Media Client's inbuilt RSS feed reader.

## Bloglovin

Bloglovin offers a very simple solution to keeping up with all the blogs you find. Bloglovin is a particularly great network for craft bloggers since it has a large creative community who are very active online, especially on Pinterest. Bloglovin users can add blogs to categorized groups and like posts by clicking on the heart symbol.

Popular posts with lots of likes are highlighted by the site, and it's easy to find new blogs and blog posts using the search function. You can also see all the posts you have liked in the past, which enables you to use this as a way of bookmarking posts to read at a later date if the introduction looks interesting.

I can find beautiful images to pin to my Pinterest boards and share links to my Twitter and Facebook accounts all without leaving Bloglovin. I advise creating clear groups of blogs so you can keep on top of blog reading – do this in the same way you curate Twitter lists.

# Inspiring content resources

» **Pinterest**
Pinterest is a particularly excellent resource for finding shareable content. I regularly follow (and unfollow) boards on Pinterest in order to keep my Pinterest feed full of only highly relevant posts. Cutting away the noise and being left with streams of fantastic and inspiring content will do just that – inspire you!

» **Facebook**
If you find Facebook pages that have consistently inspiring content, for example, a page on nature photography that you find really creative, then be sure to click on the page settings to get notifications from this page. If they only post sporadically, then this means you will never miss a post because Facebook will alert you.

» **Twitter**
As we discussed previously, Twitter lists are a great way of honing down specific people to network with, but you can also create lists of people who share links and content that you enjoy. Check Twitter lists daily and you will never be short of content to retweet or content that you can share on other networks. Why not tag the Twitter user on one of their other networks when you share – a great way to connect!

» **Google Search**
Most of us now rely on Google for finding information, but the vast majority just type their search in and look at the top results. Learn to use Google more effectively so you can find exactly the relevant content you need.

### JAMIE CHALMERS, MR X STITCH

For me it's about curation: finding interesting content and artists online and connecting with them so that I can feature their work. I use Hootsuite as a way of processing Twitter feeds, with specific searches set up, and then I also use Feedly to go through RSS feeds. My best results come from some of the art Tumblr blogs I follow, which will often feature textile artists I've never seen before.

*I advise creating clear groups of blogs so you can keep on top of blog reading – do this in the same way you curate Twitter lists.*

Scan through posts in your Bloglovin or other RSS feed and click 'like' on any that catch your eye. There is never enough time to read every blog, so creating groups of top blogs for particular topics is incredibly useful for saving time.

You can encourage people to follow your own blog on Bloglovin or subscribe to your RSS feed through adding a badge in your blog's sidebar/header area – just as you add social sharing icons. It's a good idea to regularly invite people on all of your social networks to follow your blog in this way – your posts will be more likely to be seen by them if you are connected on more than one channel.

# Filtering Google image results

Google image search is a fantastic tool that I use on a daily basis. You can discover fantastic blogs and resources by filtering the image search using the drop-down 'search tools' tab. Use these filters to make your search more effective:

» **Colour**
Great for creating colour themed Pinterest boards that look stunning when embedded in a blog post.

» **Size**
You will find that if you search for larger images, you often get better-quality results.

» **Type**
Search by face, photo, clipart, line-drawn or animated. Perfect for finding a specific image to illustrate a post.

» **Time**
Find the most recent photos from an event, for example.

» **Usage rights**
This allows you to find images that are free for you to use and adapt.

*You can discover fantastic blogs and resources by filtering the image search using the drop-down 'search tools' tab.*

## Using images

If you are using an image, you should always credit the owner. Look for their contact details on their website and email them if you are unsure how to do this. Many bloggers have a little section that states how they would like you to notify or credit them for using their images – keep an eye out for this in their sidebars before using an image. If anyone ever asks you to remove an image or link, do so without question.

## Google search operators and filters

You can filter web results by country, location or time as well as a few other filters. Google recently dropped some of the best filters I used to use, including being able to search just for blogs and discussions (let's hope they are reinstated). However, you can still find this information by using carefully worded search queries; this will also work with an image search.

You can also use the Advanced Search page to create these searches. Similar to searching on Twitter, use the following operators to improve your search results when using Google.

| | | |
|---|---|---|
| **Search for an exact word or phrase** | **'search'** | When searching use quotation marks around text for an exact phrase. For example, 'uk craft blogs' will return results that only contain exactly these words in exactly this order. |
| **Exclude a word or website** | **-** | By adding a minus sign immediately before a keyword or website in your search query, Google will ignore any results that contain the keyword or come from that website. You can add multiple negative keywords to further refine results.<br><br>**Handmade Stationery -wedding**<br><br>**Tana Lawn -ebay.com -ebay.co.uk** |
| **Search within a site or domain** | **site:** | Filter results so that they only come from a particular website, or a domain.<br><br>This is really useful for searching for Blogspot or Wordpress blogs posting about a particular subject.<br><br>**craft site:blogspot.co.uk** |
| **Search for pages that link to a URL** | **link:** | You can use this to find web pages that link to a site – this is really useful when you find a site within your niche because it will give you a list of lots of other sites that may also be ukcraftblog.com.<br><br>**link:ukcraftblog.com** |
| **Search for pages that are similar to a URL** | **related:** | This is a very useful operator as it offers up sites similar to a site you already know – again, great for building up your lists of blogs to follow and bloggers/influencers to network with. Also good for finding sites similar to your own.<br><br>**related:ukcraftblog.com** |

| | | |
|---|---|---|
| Fill in the blank | * | Adding an asterisk gives you results that contain the words you search for plus a blank – this can be a fun way of finding interesting sites.<br><br>beautiful * crafts |
| Search for either word | OR | When you use two words in a search Google will tend to show results that contain both words (this is why keywords and keyword order is so important in SEO). Use OR (capitalized) in order to get the best results that contain either word.<br><br>Knitting OR Crochet tutorials |
| Find site information in one place | info: | A quick way to find links to the cached version of a site or web page, similar pages and pages that link to the site.<br><br>info:ukcraftblog.com |
| See a cached version of a site | cache: | With this operator you can find what a page looks like the last time Google crawled the site. Useful for quickly checking if Google has crawled your website since your last post.<br><br>cache:ukcraftblog.com |

## Google Alerts

Head to Google Alerts http://www.google.co.uk/alerts in order to set up notifications for any sites that create content that matches certain keywords. Don't use terms that are too broad or you will be flooded with information and never have time to read it, leaving you feeling overwhelmed. Keep alerts close to your subjects.

By using alerts, you may be the first to share and comment on some interesting content and that will give you 'influencer' status and see your posts more likely to be shared.

It's great to add in your own site as a Google alert so you can head over to the site that has mentioned you and say thanks – often, people are too busy to bother to tweet or email you when they share your work, even if they add a link. Try not to make this mistake yourself because letting people know you have featured them by tagging or emailing them is a great way to network with influencers.

# WHERE AND WHEN TO SHARE CONTENT

You can share interesting articles and images by retweeting, reposting or repinning or you can bookmark a link or an image for use later. Perhaps you will use it as inspiration for a future blog post, or to add a comment or to tweet the blogger as part of your networking strategy. I try to do research for my clients all in one batch for the week and so I need to have a stash of useful content that I can call on when scheduling their weekly updates. This is great for time saving!

Private Pinterest boards can be really useful for saving content for use later when you have time or for researching blog posts. Alternatively, sign up for a free bookmarking service, such as pocket.com, which allows you to very quickly add a link or Facebook post and a tag so you can find it later when you are looking for content to share.

## Time management

It may be that you work full time and only have weekends, or that you work around caring for young children. Whatever your situation, dedicate a set period of time every week for research and writing. Forward planning will save you time! Posting 'on the fly' can be great for creating timely posts, but as your business grows you need to be concentrating on producing your products and packing up orders. Making your marketing research part of your weekly activity in one block will produce far more effective results than spending 10 or 15 minutes on it here and there.

That said, you still need to log in to your accounts regularly to ensure you are answering any questions and taking part in live networking. You will naturally find links and images to save for later or reshare as you are networking.

*Forward planning will save you time!*

## DON'T BE A ROBOT!

Curating content should not be mechanical. While it is fine to use time-saving tools and schedule content in advance, you still need to add your unique voice (or that of your brand) to everything you share.

This is where your creativity comes in and what makes the difference between a robot spewing out related content and YOU, an intelligent and creative person, someone who is passionate about your subject and lets that shine through. This is why people will follow your news feeds and how you become an influencer in your own right.

*Creating a cross-channel content strategy*

# AUTO SHARING CONTENT

While I generally don't encourage the overuse of auto posting or sharing the same content across different networks with differing types of users, when time is precious I think there is a place for it. If the alternative is not having a presence on a network then I positively encourage it.

It is possible with most networks to pick and choose which 'type' of posts are auto shared to other networks. For example, you can share every Facebook post directly to Twitter or just choose to share posts with links, or posts with no links.

The one caveat to auto sharing content is that you must respond to messages and comments received on a network where you are duplicating content; otherwise you will be seen as unprofessional and uninterested. Make sure that checking replies and comments is an important part of your social networking schedule. The last thing you want is to work hard creating interesting and engaging content but to ignore those people who take the time to share or comment on your posts.

## Social media and Twitter clients

Social media management tools and Twitter clients allow you to streamline your activity on Twitter and other sites. There are many available. The more social media becomes an essential part of online marketing, the more services to help make this easier pop up, each proclaiming bigger and better features to help with your networking.

These management tools are designed for people who are involved in social media marketing as opposed to using networks such as Twitter for fun, and they aim to make your networking time more efficient. Most of these services offer a free basic account and you get more features when you pay.

## Auto sharing on social networks

» **Facebook**
Auto share Facebook posts to Twitter https://www.facebook.com/twitter/ Select which types of posts you will share automatically to Twitter.

» **Twitter**
You can auto share Twitter posts to Facebook https://twitter.com/settings/profile
Scroll to the bottom to set up. I advise taking great caution with this auto share because the Facebook algorithm will not like masses of tweets pasted all over your page.

» **LinkedIn**
www.linkedin.com/settings/?modal=nsettings-twitter-accounts
For setting up Twitter accounts on LinkedIn
You can toggle this option on and off with each post.

» **Pinterest**
https://pinterest.com/settings/
You can set up posts to auto share to Twitter, Facebook and Google+. Scroll to the bottom to set these up. You can auto post everything to Facebook, but I recommend doing this on a post-by-post basis, using the little share boxes available when creating your tweet, or you will flood Facebook with activity and that can damage your post reach.

» **Instagram**
With Instagram you can add accounts to share to and select accounts at the time to share with. Currently you can share to Twitter, Facebook, Flickr, Tumblr, Foursquare and some other networks but not to Pinterest or Google+.

» **Google+**
Currently there is no official automatic sharing enabled from Google+.

## BENEFITS OF A GOOD SOCIAL MEDIA CLIENT SERVICE

» Multiple social media accounts can be monitored from one 'dashboard'.
» Quick response to replies.
» Audible notifications when you receive a new mention.
» Twitter Searches can be included as a stream of information as a column, so you can keep up to date with tweets containing certain keywords.
» Twitter Lists can be included as a column so you can keep track of recent tweets from influencers, customers or whoever is included in your various lists.
» RSS Feeds help you to keep up to date with blogs you follow.
» With some clients, you can design your own dashboard, allowing you to see the most important information easily, often in multiple columns of tweets.
» You can schedule posts.
» Share posts to multiple networks at once.
» Add notes to social media accounts to flag them as people to network with or with salient customer information you need to remember.
» Create useful reports and look at post analytics.

The panel, Benefits of a Good Social Media Client Service, lists the advantages of using a social media client. Social media clients are always adding new features and finding ways to help you engage with and grow your network of fans and followers. Note that not all social media accounts I have discussed are covered by these services. Google 'Social Media Clients' to see the latest reviews to find a client that suits your needs best.

Not all benefits apply to all services, but here are a few to look out for when selecting a social media client service:

## A NOTE ABOUT FACEBOOK

Owing to the sensitive nature of the Facebook news feed algorithm, I have some concerns about using third-party services to post content to Facebook. Historically, I have found posts do better when I post directly to Facebook.

## Hootsuite

Founded in 2008, Hootsuite offers management for Facebook, Twitter, Google+ and LinkedIn and is by far the most popular of all management tools available, having grown alongside the networks themselves. Read the Hootsuite quick start guide to get started:

https://help.hootsuite.com/entries/21626925-Quick-Start-Guide

## Tweetdeck

Tweetdeck is owned by Twitter and offers you more advanced management of your Twitter account, particularly the monitoring of multiple feeds all at once: tweetdeck.twitter.com

## IFTTT – If this then that!

At https://ifttt.com, this is a fantastic website for connecting accounts and 'activities' within your social networking. It enables you to create social sharing 'recipes' where one social action triggers another. It is a valuable time saver and you can create some really useful triggers. There are many applications and networks signed up to the service, giving an almost infinite number of recipes that you can create to suit your craft business.

First you choose the 'IF' trigger from the various accounts, and IFTTT provides the options available for each site. You then choose the 'THAT', the consequence of the trigger action.

For example, you can create a recipe where 'If' you favourite a tweet it automatically saves it to the pocket.com bookmarking service, shares it on your Tumblr blog or creates a draft post on your Blogger blog.

It can take a bit of time to get used to this site but it is worth browsing through as there are some amazing little time-saving recipes! You can also browse other people's recipes, a fun way to find some time-saving automated actions.

### JAMIE CHALMERS, MR X STITCH

Use IFTTT.com to automate your outputs - it's the best thing ever!

## Sproutsocial

Personally, I use a paid service from www.sproutsocial.com for my social networking and social media management. I look after many accounts for my clients and I have found this service the best for my needs.

Paying for a management service is not necessary when you are starting out and have just one online profile to manage, but as your business grows it's worth investigating the features offered when you upgrade. The adage is true – you get what you pay for!

## Sharing Posts from Google+

As I mentioned, there are no official sharing options for Google+ yet. However, if you find you like the Google+ platform, try the Friends+ website www.friendsplus.me for automatically sharing the content you create there to Facebook, Twitter, Linkedin or Tumblr.

This site has a lot of great features, allowing you to stagger the spreading of content to other networks, and currently has a free plan for smaller accounts. Ensuring you are posting to Google+ is potentially beneficial to your search ranking (see 'The essentials of content marketing'). It is a good idea to use Google+ as a content generator, posting original content here first that is then reshared with other sites. As always, take care not to annoy the algorithm when sharing with Facebook.

# NEWSLETTERS

One of the key goals of your social media marketing for your business is to build up a database of newsletter subscribers and customers that you can email regularly to keep them up to date with your latest blog posts, offers and promotions.

## Why send a regular newsletter?

Newsletters belong to you. Unlike social media networks, you are not renting the platform, you own it. This is the way you can connect directly with your subscribers, keeping your crafts and, importantly, your brand in the minds of people who, with the right strategy, will eventually convert and buy.

Converting social media follows and likes into subscribers is key to building a successful craft business. As your database grows, so does your chance of selling your work and building a following of fans who are keen to see your latest designs and ideas.

Your subscribers won't buy from you every time you send a newsletter, but by sending a newsletter you will keep your products in the minds of people when they want to buy a gift or treat. Your job is to work out how to keep your newsletter readers engaged, so that when they are ready to buy, they buy from you – a trusted brand they have grown to respect.

## Setting up your newsletter

Choose a quality newsletter provider. There are many available (search for Google 'Newsletter providers'). I find www.mailchimp.com works really well for me and has lots of great features for free accounts while you are building up numbers.

Opening an account with Mailchimp is very straightforward and you can easily import your existing lists of subscribers just by copying and pasting from a spreadsheet or uploading a file.

Mailchimp also allows you to easily create professional-looking templates using 'drag and drop', so you can add and edit images, sidebars with quick links to your website, text and social icons. You can add in links, text and images based around the content you have been sharing and your latest pieces.

## POLLY DOUGDALE, HANDMADE HORIZONS

Including a newsletter sign-up form on your site is a great way to keep in touch with customers who might not be ready to buy straight away. A well-timed newsletter containing an offer or news of a new product launch will remind them that you exist and could be what they need to persuade them that they must have the item that tempted them before!

## Tips for creating a quality newsletter

### Frequency

Decide on how regularly you can send out a newsletter. If you are sharing at least two to three good-quality blog posts a week, then you can probably send a post every week because you have enough content to share.

Many people find that a monthly round-up works well. The key thing is try to be consistent with the frequency and tone of your newsletter so that people get used to seeing and opening your emails.

### Bring all your content together in your newsletter

Your newsletter needs to be interesting – it sounds obvious, but unless you email people with useful, interesting or humorous information they will soon unsubscribe or simply stop bothering to open your emails.

Don't assume your subscribers will already have read all your content. Chances are they won't have seen your tweets and social media posts.

Most companies look to their blog and create a round-up of the top posts alongside salient news of any offers or competitions. As an independent, you can add in much more personality, perhaps opening with a recap of your recent blog posts or something interesting to get people's attention. Ensure that the subject matter matches the first few sentences of your post. If you have mentioned an offer, make sure it is visible the moment they open the newsletter as a header image or sidebar image, even if you go into more detail further down.

Keep the content light and be concise. If you are linking to a blog post give a sentence below an image from the post to explain why the reader should click through to read more.

In addition, you can share Pinterest boards you have created or followed, blogs you have recently followed or any number of mentions of interesting and relevant people and blogs that you are keen to share. Your readers will soon start to rely on your newsletter being a choppy mix of all the fun content they are probably too busy to find themselves, alongside your posts and of course, details of your latest products and shop listings.

A great way of networking is to tag someone on a social network to say 'I've linked to your blog in my latest newsletter!' Mailchimp creates an online version of your newsletter, just like a web page, so you can share the newsletter on all of your social networks.

Your newsletter can be a catalyst for your weekly content creation because by creating a template you know what 'slots' you need to fill. Be sure to add this into your posting schedule. With a newsletter you become the editor of your own company magazine – a magazine that perfectly fits your target market because it is a culmination of all of your marketing and networking online.

Getting someone to subscribe may seem like the biggest hurdle, but sadly it isn't! The real test is creating a newsletter that people open.

> With a newsletter you become the editor of your own company magazine – a magazine that perfectly fits your target market because it is a culmination of all of your marketing and networking online.

## Measuring newsletter success

Mailchimp has a fantastic report centre that allows you to see the open rate (the number of people who open your email) and the number of clicks on links within the newsletter. Be sure to add Google Analytics tracking information when creating your email so you can track the success of your links by looking at the behaviour of your subscribers when on your website. For example, you can see in your analytics whether a reader who clicked on your latest blog post link immediately clicked away or whether they clicked through for more information elsewhere on your site. As these visitors have already signed up to your newsletter, the next step is to get them to buy or share. You can track whether or not someone took up an offer and the percentage of these people that came from your newsletter. This will give you a way of measuring the return on investment of all the hard work you are doing building up your mailing lists. If newsletter subscribers tend to have a higher conversion rate than social media fans and followers, it is worth putting more effort into building these lists.

# Top tips to get people to open your newsletter

» **Timing**
Think about the most appropriate time to send your newsletter. Remember that many emails remain unopened days after they arrive as we all have busy lives, and emails from friends and colleagues take priority. Consider when people in your target market are most likely to be online. You might like to send at lunchtime to catch people having a lunch break or perhaps in the evening after parents have put their children to bed. If you look at your Facebook Insights (in the Page Admin area) you will see data for when your posts do best – you could use this information to decide on a good time to send your newsletter.

» **Subject line**
The subject line needs to make people click, so think hard about how you can tempt people to open. If you have an offer available, make it sound unmissable. If you don't have an offer or competition to tempt people with, then you need to think of a

question or statement to get people opening:

'How do you...'
'The best way to...'
'Learn how to...'

» **Personal approach**
Even better is to use your own voice and talk in the first person! This makes your newsletter feel like a more personal email. With Mailchimp you can also easily add merge tags, which allows you to use people's first names in the text.

» **Use humour and drama**
Your brand identity and your unique angle on the world need to come through in a subject line. You are not a huge company spamming your followers with emails about offers – you're the real person behind the brand with interesting stories to tell. Humour and drama work! Try these openers:

'How I coped with...'
'The newsletter where I tell you about...'
'Is this my best ever...?'
'Why I decided to...'
'Could this be my worst/best...?'

# IS IT ALL WORKING?

Measuring your success may feel a little like the conclusion to all your efforts of online marketing, but you shouldn't think of it this way. Measuring the success and failures of your marketing efforts should be a part of your process. If you don't set goals you won't be able to analyse success, and without an understanding of how to analyse and what you can analyse, you can't set realistic and measurable goals.

You need to give the people you are marketing and selling your products to the best experience you can by creating a funnel that starts with social media networking and content marketing and ends with a particular outcome – the buying of your beautiful crafts and designs. This is the way to ensure they tell all their friends about you!

Acquisition for me is the fun part where you cast a net to find potential new customers and people who may share your brand. However, the B and C of behaviour and conversion are the difference between a craft business that opportunistically floats along the river without a real direction, and a business that is climbing steadily up the mountain because it sets measurable goals and objectives for each day, week, month and year.

As a creative person you have all the skills necessary to get people interested; you just need the tools to know if you are succeeding. Understanding analytics gives you this knowledge. I apply this principle to everything that I do for my clients, from a post on Facebook that takes minutes, to a post on their blog that can take hours of research. You need to do the same with your business.

# GOOGLE ANALYTICS

Google Analytics can measure and analyse visits to your websites. All computers have a unique IP address. Through tracking each address, it is possible to know how many times a person has visited your blog or website, how long they stayed and exactly what they looked at and clicked on.

You can also see how a user found your site, whether from another site or through a search engine with a specific keyword. Other web analytics tools exist but Google Analytics is excellent and it is free.

Don't expect to immediately understand all the measurements or 'metrics' available on Google Analytics. It takes time to learn and some are very complex and multi-layered. Google has some brilliant video tutorials in the help section of the site that I strongly recommend you take time to watch.

## Help

You will need this! The Analytics reports are vast and can be overwhelming. In the top corner of all of your reports you will see a little mortar board, which will give you advice on every element of your Google Analytics reports.

To follow is a very simple overview of a few features of Google Analytics that I find most useful, which will help you to get started with measuring your content marketing efforts online. It is by no means a complete guide. Google has that wrapped up in its extensive help guides and videos, which are regularly updated as new features and metrics emerge. These tools provide enormously useful information for tracking the health of your website.

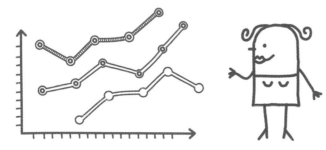

## How to install Google Analytics

» **Follow this link** http://www.google.com/analytics/ Install the tracking code into your site if you do not already have Analytics. There are instructions for every stage and plenty of advice and tips for understanding the Analytics available.

» **Set up the Webmaster Tools on Google Analytics.** Go to www.google.com/webmasters/tools Google will again take you through this process.

## Using Webmaster Tools you can:

» **Find details on how Google is crawling your site** You will find out if there are any broken links.

» **Look at traffic data, including search queries and impressions (how many times your results came up in the search for a particular query)** It shows you how many people searched for the term, how many clicked on your result and also your average ranking position for the term. You may be ranked number one for lots of keyword phrases but if no one is searching or clicking through, they are not worth a great deal to your marketing campaign.

» **Check inbound links** These are all the sites with a link through to your website.

» **Check optimization data** This is data, including content keywords, that Google has found on your site.

## Set up e-commerce tracking

If you sell direct from your site, this feature is an excellent way of seeing how web traffic converts directly to sales. Ensure that in your Analytics admin settings you have e-commerce tracking switched on. Use the help pages on Google Analytics for further tips on setting up e-commerce tracking correctly – you may need a website designer. If you use a third-party shopping basket, such as an e-commerce plug-in, you should refer to the help area to ensure you set up the e-commerce Analytics correctly.

## Google Analytics reports

When you open your Analytics, you will be presented with the report's view; this is an overview of the last month of activity on your site in graph form and some general metrics below.

On all reports you can change the date range and also toggle the granularity, choosing hour, day, week or month and you can also compare the data with previous periods. This is great for quickly looking at the health of your site compared to the previous month or the same month the previous year.

## Delve deeper into Google Analytics

You need to delve a little deeper to see which aspects of your marketing activity are the most successful. As I have mentioned throughout this book, the key performance indicators are Acquisition, Behaviour and Conversion. All of these aspects of your marketing can be measured using Google Analytics.

# Google Analytics – metrics

» **Sessions**
A session is the period of time that a visitor is engaged with your site (previously called 'visit'). The longer they stay, the better in most cases because it means they are engaged with your content and not simply clicking away after they reach the page from a referring link, one of your social networks or from a search.

» **Users**
A user is a person who has had at least one session within the selected date range. A user historically was referred to as a 'unique page view'. The more users the better!

» **Pageviews**
This is the total number of pages on your site that have been viewed by all users. If there are lots of pageviews, it suggests that people are engaged with your content. This does of course depend on which pages they are viewing – they could be flipping back and forth between pages looking for information they don't ever find.

» **Pages/Session**
Sometimes referred to as 'average page depth', this is the number of pages on your website viewed during each session, which allows you to see how engaged the average user is with your site. A higher number means people are clicking around the various pages on your site looking at more products or more blog posts.

» **Average Session Duration**
This is how long a session lasts on average. Longer sessions tend to show a healthier page because it suggests people are staying and reading the content thoroughly.

» **Bounce rate**
This is the number of single-page views. In general, a high bounce rate suggests that you have not met a particular goal. For example, on a blog post your goal may be to get a visitor to click through to a page where you share details of a new design. If they do not click and simply go back to where they came from, this will be recorded as a bounce. A bounce does not mean they clicked away quickly as the name suggests, though. (In fact, I wouldn't be surprised if Google renames this metric because it often causes confusion.) If the goal was to send your visitor to your Etsy Shop from a direct link then a high bounce rate is not a bad thing.

» **New and returning sessions**
This is an important 'general' metric because it instantly tells you how many of the visitors to your site were visiting for the first time. This shows if you are reaching out to potential new customers with your content and also if you are keeping existing users engaged enough that they are returning to see more content.

An increasing number of return visitors suggests that your marketing efforts are paying off. It's not all about new users, although of course you need new visitors to grow your returning users figure!

## Setting up goals

In the admin section of Google Analytics you can set up specific goals that relate to certain activities of visitors to your website. Just click on goals and 'Add Goal' to start. Setting up goals early on in your marketing campaign will help keep you focused and save you time when looking at reports.

The goals you choose depend on your business objectives. Google Analytics takes you through the process step by step, enabling you to set particular goals to suit your online marketing. These goals are then accessible in your reports, allowing you to see which of your marketing efforts is most successful and using this to improve and tweak your strategy.

For example, using goals you could find that people who visit from Pinterest rarely stay for longer than two minutes or sign up to your newsletter and yet they represent the majority of your social traffic.

Setting up a goal could help you to optimize popular pages that Pinterest users are visiting by adding a bigger call to action on a particular blog post to sign up for further great content. This then becomes a goal that you can track easily using Google Analytics by just clicking on this particular 'Newsletter Sign Up' goal you have set up to see if your optimization has increased the number of pinners subscribing to your newsletter.

# Goal types

You can set up to 20 goals in your Analytics, which is plenty for most small businesses. Google gives you template goals that you may find confusing. However, if you click on 'custom' you can simply set up goals for your own needs and you will be given the following four objectives.

» **1 Destination**
This is the goal I use most! Click on Destination to set up a goal for when a visitor ends up at a specific page on your site. This could be a newsletter sign-up page or any important page on your site defined by your own business objectives. An important page could be a page called http://yourwebsite.com/shop where you list all the stockists of your products. All you need to do is add the /shop part of the address when prompted.

» **2 Duration**
A goal that shows that a visitor stays on your site for a certain amount of time could indicate that they are carefully reading content from your site. The longer people are on your site, the better. Your goal could be to ensure that visitors spend two minutes on your site. Do these visitors tend to go on to buy or to share your content?

» **3 Pages per visit**
You can set up a goal that shows you how engaged a visitor is on your site by measuring how deeply they look around.

» **4 Event**
Event tracking, for example, clicking on an advert or app needs an experienced developer to set up.

## Adding funnels

Within the goal set-up pages you can also add a funnel, or path. This is a way of setting up a path for how people will get to the destination. Head to Google's help pages for more information about using this feature.

## Segments

In addition to setting up goals you can also create segments, which allow you to focus on specific types of users. You can segment users based on age, location, first-time visitors and more. Click on segments in the admin area to set these up.

Again, you should experiment with segments only once you have mastered the basics of understanding reports. It can be extremely useful to quickly access your saved segments. For example, if you only ship within your own country you can segment data by country, eliminating the traffic from countries that cannot buy from you. You can then look at strategies for increasing user numbers from your target country (or city) by thinking up more localized blog content campaigns.

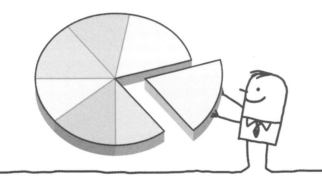

## Acquisition – clicks!

Acquisition in terms of building a social media following is to increase your likes and follows. Within Analytics, acquisition relates directly to clicks through to your website and where they came from.

Click on 'Acquisition' in reports, which enables you to see people who have clicked to your website in the following ways. Click on each for further detailed information.

**Social**
**Referral**
**Email**
**Direct**
**Organic**

You will also see that you have information from the goals you have set up automatically in your reports. You can use the drop-down goals tab to see specific goals and the percentage of visits from that metric that resulted in a goal completion, instantly giving you data on what is working and what is not! You can ask yourself the following questions:

Which of your channels is doing best to bring in clicks and help you to complete your goals?

Has your networking with influencers been successful? If you have spent time writing a guest post for a site you can see in referral traffic the specific number of clicks and how many were new visits. This will help you decide if it's worth building on this relationship and looking to write more.

"**Which of your channels is doing best to bring in clicks and help you to complete your goals**"

## Behaviour

Look at the Behaviour section of Google Analytics reports to see how people are interacting with your content. This is where you want to try to lead people in a certain direction on your site, preferably to your products or newsletter sign-up.

### Turn the clicks into customers or subscribers!

If a post from your blog is doing well, can it be further optimized and kept up to date by adding in links to other areas of your site? Look at the bounce rate and new visitors rate, for example. Are they very high, indicating people are reading the content and leaving?

If the traffic is all coming from one referral, bear in mind the type of visitor and their interests. What could you tempt them with to stay a little longer and have a look around your site? Perhaps you could add links within the text or at the end of the post to related content on your site.

Think about why a blog post is getting more traffic than others and try to build on its success rather than smiling away at the number of visitors. Can you expand on the content with a new post? Could you approach a magazine editor in your niche area and offer to write something similar, letting them know how popular the post has been within your own readership?

Conversely, do you have posts that are performing badly with not much traffic being acquired from any sources? Could you improve the images? Perhaps you could look to promote the post further by sharing it with an influencer you think could be interested or simply resharing it on your channels with a few tweaks and changes to improve it.

If you change the title of a post in most blogging platforms, the URL, or 'permalink', will remain the same, leaving any inbound links intact but giving you the opportunity to try a more catchy title.

---

### Google Analytics Behaviour

In this section you can analyse:

» **Site content**
All the pages on your site and the behaviour and type of users visiting

» **Landing pages**
The pages people arrive at on your site – useful for looking at which landing pages lead to the best goal outcomes.

» **Exit pages**
Where people leave your site – useful for determining if a page needs further optimization and tweaking to lead people towards a goal. Exit pages aren't always bad; it could be you have a high exit rate from a page that is sharing a product you have listed for sale on an online marketplace, for example. You will see which pages are performing best with the most visitors when you open up the report overview, or click on 'All Pages' in the site content section.

---

## Conversion

In this area of Google Analytics reports you can track the important conversions, your custom goals, and also e-commerce.

Here you will also find the Assisted Conversions tab, which allows you to track any sales that have indirectly come via social media – useful for understanding more fully how your social media activity is drawing customers. People may not buy directly after finding you via that Facebook post but you can track if they return up to 30 days later, and Facebook will be given the 'assist'. If they subsequently sign up to your newsletter, the sales revenue will be split between the two.

With this information from Google Analytics, you will have enough understanding to know what you want to learn more about. You can even gain a qualification from Google Analytics by working through all the training videos, showing you just how much there is to learn. If you are interested search 'Analytics IQ', where you can sign up.

The important thing is not to dismiss Analytics as too complicated. Break it down into the three important 'ABC' sections and you will soon start to find it increasingly more interesting to set up goals and delve even deeper into the many reports available.

# CONCLUSION

At first, it doesn't matter if you feel like you are only getting 'likes' from fellow crafters. This is not a negative when you are starting out building your following on social media channels – it's a huge positive! These are your messengers, the people who will spread the word about your work through their blogs and social networks. They have the collective potential to get your work spotted by influential editors! Don't think, 'Who are these people?' Instead think, 'Who else follows these people?'

**?** *"Only crafty people 'like' me – how will that increase my sales"*

Don't think of it as preaching to the converted when you network with fellow crafters, think of it as giving the converted a bunch of leaflets to deliver all round the village and beyond! People who love craft love to not only buy handmade items, but also tell all their friends about them.

If you are making fellow crafters smile, click or share, then your social media marketing is positively reinforcing your brand identity. You will see this effect through increased sales and web traffic and also more emails and tweets from influential sites and editors of publications who are keen to feature your work.

A feature or design in a craft magazine or top craft blog can lead to your work being spotted by journalists and lifestyle magazines outside of the craft industry.

Using the tools and tactics you have learnt from reading this book, you can network with bloggers and influencers from all kinds of complementary businesses outside the craft industry. Grow your reach beyond the craft market and you will start to see your posts being shared by the people who have a direct influence over your potential customers.

# What to do next

Thank you for reading through to the end of my book. I hope you are inspired and feeling like your business is full of potential! The following points are important to remember and are a summary of the most essential aspects of online marketing.

» If you don't know who your market is, your sales will be sporadic and your craft business will not grow!

» Always have a goal in mind whenever you post an update to a social media network or to your blog.

» Carry a camera everywhere and learn how to take high-quality, bright, in-focus pictures.

» Plan ahead to avoid burnout and 'blogger's block'; resenting the time you are spending marketing is not healthy for your craft business.

» Measure your results.

» Eat, sleep, tweet, repeat – get online as often as you can but don't get addicted!

You cannot overestimate the impact of feeling on top of your online marketing work. It will make you more confident, more proactive and will have a positive effect on every single aspect of your business.

**If you have any questions please contact me @craftbloguk on Twitter.**

Hilary Pullen

## SARAH CORBETT, CRAFTIVIST COLLECTIVE

**You have to believe that your business is something needed by others in our world and that you are the only person with the unique mix of skills, experience and passion to lead your business. People will be attracted to your passion, belief and unique voice, which will help them become long-term supporters, customers and champions of your business.**

# GLOSSARY

**@mention**
A tagged mention. Using @ works on Twitter, Google+, Instagram and Facebook – type @ followed by the first few letters of the person you want to tag, and they will be notified of your post.

**above the fold**
What people see when they land on your page; anything below the fold isn't immediately obvious so put important calls to action and information above the fold.

**algorithm**
A set of rules that is followed to give a particular outcome; both the Google search engine and Facebook have an algorithm to determine what is shown in the search results or news feed.

**Analytics**
Tools to measure your success on various platforms in terms of number of clicks and links in from other sites. Also invaluable for looking at the behaviour of people when they visit your website.

**API**
Application Programming Interface – a set of functions and procedures that allow the creation of applications which access the features or data of an operating system, application or other service. For example, Hootsuite uses the Twitter API to access details so it can offer you information on your account activity.

**authenticity**
An attribute you need to be trustworthy and sincere when social networking – being authentic will pay huge dividends because your audience will trust and respect you. You cannot pay for this; it has to be earned.

**avatar**
The graphical representation of a person's alter ego or character on a social network – the profile picture which accompanies all your comments and that you use on your social networking accounts.

**B2B**
Business to Business – as opposed to Business to Consumer. We talk about B2B networking where you create connections with other complementary businesses that could help to build awareness of your own brand through mutually beneficial promotions.

**backlink**
A link from another site that when clicked goes to your site.

**Bitly**
A link-shortening service that also gives analytics on link clicks.

**blog**
A website which is updated regularly with the most recent post first. Many companies now attach a blog to their website to share news and to create content which will help them to be found in a search. Individuals often use a blog as an online diary.

**Blogger**
Owned by Google, an online blogging platform.

**blogosphere**
The world of interconnected bloggers.

**bookmark**
To add a website page to a list so that you can find and read/share it later. Bookmarking is available through your browser or you can set up profiles on bookmark services to share your content.

**brand advocate**
A super-fan that regularly shares and comments publicly on your posts.

**browser**
A software application, such as Internet Explorer, Firefox or Google Chrome, which allows you to surf the Internet. Make sure your browser is up to date because an outdated browser can cause many problems when looking at websites.

**categories**
Blog posts are divided into categories on some blogging platforms such as Wordpress – this allows you to organize your blog posts so that content can be found easily.

**chat**
If anyone ever refers to online chatting or Facebook chats they tend to mean using an instant messaging service, which is private only for the individuals involved in the chat. It can be useful for networking outside a social network to discuss an issue in depth. Skype or Facebook messenger are both good examples of online chat facilities.

**circle**
Google+ uses circles as a way to compartmentalize people you are following so that you can follow the activity of specific groups of people and pages.

**click**
When someone clicks on any link on a website, it is recorded by your analytics so you can see the activity of people on your website, and also the link on the site that they clicked on to find your website.

**CMS**
Content management system, such as the blogging programme Wordpress.

**comment**
A comment someone leaves on your blog posts or social media posts.

**content**
Any text, image, video or audio post that appears on the Internet and on websites is considered to be content.

**content marketing**
A way of bringing people to your site or social media accounts by posting relevant content that can be found through a search engine.

**conversion**
Any activity on your site or social media channels that results in someone completing one of your predefined goals, such as buying a product or signing up to your mailing list.

**CPC (Cost Per Click)**
A widely used system of paying for advertising where you only pay when someone actually clicks, rather than paying for people just to see your advert or promotion.

**Creative Commons**
Creative Commons is a non-profit organization headquartered in Mountain View, California, United States, devoted to expanding the range of creative works available for others to build upon legally and to share.

**crowdsourcing**
A method of obtaining information or input by enlisting the services of a number of people, either paid or unpaid.

**demographic**
Statistical data relating to the population and particular groups within it.

**ebook**
An online book that people can download to read on their computer, tablet or phone.

**editorial calendar**
A calendar showing the themes and content you have planned for the coming months.

**embed**
Adding a snippet of code to a website or blogpost so that a YouTube video, tweet, Instagram picture or any other piece of online content can be shared on a website easily. Most social media sites give you the option to embed a post and create the snippet of code for you to paste into your blog posts and websites. When blogging you need to be in 'html' or 'code' view to enable you to paste in a snippet of code.

**engagement**
Any activity from readers, fans and followers, such as shares, likes, retweets or comments.

**engagement marketing**
Creating a marketing strategy with an emphasis on getting people to engage with posts and therefore allowing your site and social media channels to organically grow through word of mouth (or click, like and share).

**evergreen post**
A post that is not specific to a certain date or event and will continue to bring traffic to your blog.

**fan**
Someone who likes a Facebook page (or other social media network) and will receive your updates in their news feed.

**feed**
A web feed (or news feed) is a data format used for providing users with frequently updated content. Content distributors syndicate a web feed, allowing users to subscribe to it. Making a collection of web feeds accessible in one spot is known as aggregation.

**follow**
When someone follows you online they receive updates through a particular social media site or RSS feed.

**forum**
An Internet forum, or message board, is an online discussion site where people can hold conversations in the form of posted messages.

**friend**

On a Facebook personal profile specifically, a friend is someone who you have allowed to see your posts. When people like a Facebook Fan Page they are not a friend but a fan as you cannot see their personal profiles.

**Google Alert**

An alert set up to notify you of specific public content posted on the Internet, such as a mention of your website or a particular keyword phrase which you have identified as important to follow.

**guest post**

A blog post written by someone other than the regular author of a blog.

**hashtag**

A way of creating a hyperlink to a specific subject by adding a hashtag before a word or phrase with no spaces. People often use them to join in with public conversations online on subjects that are relevant to their business or interests and the specific post they have shared. When you click on a hashtag, a social media site such as Twitter, Instagram, Facebook or Pinterest, will create a feed of all of the people who have used the tag. If used on a private profile the post will not appear in the results.

**HTML**

Hypertext Markup Language – the code behind what you see on a website through your browser.

**hyperlink**

A link which when clicked takes you to another webpage.

**inbound link**

A link anywhere on the Internet that when clicked takes someone to your website, as opposed to an internal link, which is a link on your blog or website that takes you to another page within your site, or an external link that takes someone from your site to another site.

**influencer**

A company, person or group of people who have a niche following in an area of relevance to your business.

**instant messaging (IM)**

IM is chat on a network (such as Facebook, Skype or Google+) that offers people the ability to send messages to each other instantly to create a conversation. It is really useful when you don't want to video call or email but need something in between.

**keyword**

A descriptive word, or a phrase made up of a few words, which you have identified through research that your target market will be searching for.

**link building**

Actively working to increase the number of inbound links – links that go from another website to yours.

**longtail keyword**

A specific keyword phrase that consists of two or more words. In content marketing we use longtail keywords to target customers who are close to the purchasing stage of their search. They know exactly what they are looking for.

**lurker**

Someone who is following you online but does not comment or click. It's not a nice word, but there are far more lurkers than brand advocates!

**meme**

Online content that is copied and spread, usually with a slight variation. (A good example is the 'Keep Calm and . . .' slogan). If correctly targeted, creating, evolving or sharing a meme can be great for engagement and associating yourself with a particular group.

**newsletter**

A regular email used to bring traffic to your website that goes out to your mailing list, usually containing news, articles and offers.

**organic search**

A search which is free, rather than a person clicking on paid-for results.

**paid search**

Search traffic that has been paid for, using services such as adwords from Google.

**permalink**

The permanent web address or url of a blog post. You should always share and link to the permalink rather than the home-page address for recent blog posts because over time and with the addition of new posts, they will no longer be available on the home page.

**pillar post**

A useful post that contains links to lots of other connected posts on a particular subject. Pillar posts can all be from your own site, or a collection of posts on a topic from other sites.

**podcast**

An audio post that people can listen to. People often create series of podcasts on a weekly basis in the same way people create blogs and vlogs. The podcast can be embedded into a blog or website.

**reach**

The number of people who may have seen your content. This can be measured within a social network, for example, using Facebook Insights, or it could be measured by looking at the number of page views, retweets, repins etc and creating a cumulative figure. Reach is less useful than measuring actual engagement because just having seen a post or update does not indicate the user has actually read it. A click, share or comment is proof that the content has been read.

**RSS Feed**

Rich Site Summary/Really Simple Syndication: a web feed of the most recent updates from a website or blog, often imported into a feed reader so the user can create a magazine of all of their favourite content (for example, feedly.com).

**SEM**

Search Engine Marketing – promoting websites by increasing their visibility in search engine results pages.

**SEO**

Search Engine Optimization – the process of affecting the visibility of a website or a web page in a search engine's organic search results.

**SERPS**

Search Engine Results Pages.

**SMO**

Social Media Optimization: using social media channels and communities to generate publicity to increase the awareness of a business or product.

**social media channel**

A social network used for acquiring customers – the channel refers to the path a user takes from awareness of the brand through to conversion (buying a product).

**social share**

A person sharing content on social media to their own social network, for example, a Facebook share or a repin on Pinterest.

**status update**

Updating any social network with content, such as news, pictures or videos.

**syndication**

Making web feeds available from a site in order to provide other people with a summary or full update of the sites most recent content (via an RSS Feed).

**tag**

A label added to a blog post in order to help a reader find related content. Clicking on a tag will bring up all content that is tagged with the same word or phrase. These tags can be indexed by search engines.

**thread**

A conversation between two or more people on a public forum or social network.

**troll**

An ugly individual who delights in being troublesome online. Never 'feed the trolls' by engaging with people who are just posting to cause an argument or undermine your craft business in any way. But do not confuse trolls with people who have genuine cause for complaint.

**Tweet Chat**

A chat on Twitter at a specific time (often weekly) where people use a specific hashtag to create a conversation.

**URL**

Uniform Resource Locator – a web address such as: http://ukcraftblog.com.

**URL Shortener**

A service such as Bitly.com that will shorten your URLs so that they fit into a tweet. Links shared on Twitter.com will automatically be shortened to an http://t.co link.

**vlog**

A video blog – instead of typing your blog, you record it. Many YouTube and Vimeo users call themselves vloggers; most have an associated blog or website where they embed these videos.

**wall**

A Facebook wall where post updates can be found – people might say 'It's on my Facebook wall', meaning it's been posted to their Facebook timeline.

**webinar**

A seminar conducted over the Internet.

**widget**

A software application that is used on websites, a widget uses information gathered from another website and displays it in a particular way, usually customizable. It is also called a gadget. For example, you can add a Twitter widget to your blog sidebar that displays your latest tweets or a Pinterest widget which displays your latest pins.

# HELPFUL LINKS AND RESOURCES

Here are a few links to sites you will find useful when blogging and networking.

### Useful help pages
Social media platforms are updated so regularly with new layouts and features that it's best to go direct to the site for the basics of navigating each platform.

http://help.pinterest.com
http://support.google.com/plus
http://support.twitter.com
https://help.instagram.com
https://help.linkedin.com
https://support.google.com/youtube
www.facebook.com/help

### Dedicated picture and video sharing sites
Find and share images and videos.

http://500px.com
http://craftgawker.com
http://instagram.com
http://photobucket.com
http://pinterest.com
http://tumblr.com
http://vimeo.com
http://youtube.com
https://vine.com
http://www.flickr.com

### Bookmarking sites
Useful sites for saving, organizing and discovering web pages that can be shared on your social networks.

http://craftgawker.com
http://delicious.com
www.digg.com
http://pocket.com
www.squidoo.com
www.stumbleupon.com

### Best free social media clients
http://hootsuite.com
http://tweetdeck.twitter.com

### Free social media tools
http://bufferapp.com
Buffer spreads your posts to social networks out throughout the day or week.

http://klout.com
Klout helps you find influential people to follow.

http://topsy.com/
Helps you search and analyse social networks.

http://tweetchat.com
Find and follow specific hashtags on Twitter so you can connect with people talking about similar things. When you join Twitter Chats, it automatically adds the hashtag for you.

https://friendsplus.me
Share Google+ posts to other social networks.

### Online craft communities and forums
Forums are friendly places to chat online with crafters and add to discussions. They can be a useful way of connecting with the craft community. Most online market places also have a forum area where you can get tips from fellow shop owners.

http://craftmafia.com
http://craftstylish.com
http://craftzine.com
http://ukhandmade.ning.com
(UK members only)
www.bluecanvas.com
www.craftsforum.co.uk
www.craftster.org
www.deviantart.com
www.indiepublic.com
www.ravelry.com

### Search engine submissions
Submit your blogs and websites to these sites to help them get indexed by the search engines.

http://siteexplorer.search.yahoo.com/au/free/submit
http://technorati.com
www.bing.com/webmaster/SubmitSitePage.aspx
www.dmoz.org
www.google.com/addurl
www.pingomatic.com

# ABOUT THE AUTHOR

Hilary Pullen specializes in community management, including creating and maintaining social media accounts as well as blog editing and content writing.

She studied architecture at Plymouth University, where she developed her love of writing and research, and particularly enjoyed creating and communicating design concepts.

These skills, together with her experience working in customer service management and advertising, and her passion for creativity and craft, led her to specialize in offering her services within the craft industry.

Hilary now works with magazine publishers and crafting supplies companies, helping them to connect online with this market using the same techniques and content-marketing principles outlined in this book.

In her spare time, Hilary runs a website called Craft Blog UK, a site dedicated to supporting and celebrating the growing handmade market. She uses her experience to write and share free tips and tutorials for the successful online promotion of start-up craft businesses and to help craft bloggers build their readership.

**www.ukcraftblog.com**
**@craftbloguk**

# CONTRIBUTORS

I asked the following lovely people to contribute to this book because they are all experts at engaging with communities. Success doesn't just happen – these authors, bloggers and artists have all worked incredibly hard to get where they are now. I encourage you to connect with these brilliant people online as each and every one of them, while having shared brief tips in this book, can teach you something useful about networking and engaging with a niche market. What are you waiting for! Get on Twitter now and be sure to tell them @craftbloguk (me) says hi so I can join the conversation!

**http://cha-uk.co.uk**
*@uk_cha*
*Craig De Souza*

Craig is the director of membership services at the Craft Hobby Association, a non-profit association that exists to help businesses working in the craft industry to succeed and grow.

**http://craftivist-collective.com**
*@craftivists*
*Sarah Corbett*

Sarah is the founder of the Craftivist Collective. She works alongside individuals, charities and arts institutions, among others, to address poverty and injustice, using craft as a way of engaging, challenging and encouraging people to play their part in making the world a better place.

**http://inside-scoop.co.uk**
*@rinhamburgh*
*Rin Hamburgh*

Rin is a freelance journalist and founder of the media training company Inside Scoop.

**http://kitschycoo.blogspot.co.uk**
*@kitschycoo*
*Amanda Cusick*

Amanda runs a fabric and pattern shop selling her unique clothing designs. Her very popular blog is one of the best examples online of how blogging can help grow a business.

**http://www.handmadeology.com**
*@Handmadeology*
*Timothy Adam*

Founder of the hugely successful website handmadeology, Tim is an expert in selling handmade goods online. I was thrilled when he agreed to write the foreword for this book!

**http://lovesewingmag.co.uk**
*@LoveSewingMag*
*Helen Mclaughlin*

Helen is the editor of the popular new sewing magazine *Love Sewing*, which had such a successful launch that the first copy sold out in weeks.

http://makeanddowithperri.wordpress.com
@PerriLewis
*Perri Lewis*

Perri is the successful author of *Material World* and currently the creative director of www.mastered.com, having previously worked as a journalist, writing for the *Guardian*, *The Telegraph* and many other leading titles.

http://ukhandmade.co.uk
@kjinksdesign
*Karen Jinks*

Karen is the founder of UKHandmade, a website dedicated to supporting independent designers and craftspeople.

www.handmadehorizons.com
@Dolly_Puggles
*Polly Dougdale*

Polly is a freelance marketer who runs Handmade Horizons with Claire Hughes; they are both digital marketing experts with over twenty years' combined experience in online retail.

www.kirstyelson.co.uk
@KirstyElson
*Kirsty Elson*

Kirsty is an artist who has amassed an enormous Facebook following with over 100,000 likes.

www.molliemakes.com
@LaraMcSpara
*Lara Watson*

Lara is the editor of the magazine *Mollie Makes*, one of the most popular contemporary craft magazines on the market.

www.mrxstitch.com
@MrXStitch
*Jamie Chalmers*

Jamie writes Mr X Stitch, one of the world's best contemporary embroidery and needlecraft sites.

www.redtedart.com
@RedTedArt
*Maggy Woodley*

Maggy is the author of the successful book and blog Red Ted Art – she has more than 90,000 Pinterest followers!

www.thedesigntrust.co.uk
@TheDesignTrust
*Patricia van der Akker*

Patricia is the director of The Design Trust, an organization that helps professional designers and craftspeople to create and run better businesses.

www.thesewingdirectory.co.uk
@SewingDirectory
*Fiona Pullen*

Fiona runs The Sewing Directory and has recently written a book called *How to Craft a Creative Business*.

www.tillyandthebuttons.com
@TillyButtons
*Tilly Waines*

Tilly is the author of *Love at First Stitch* and writes a very successful sewing blog. She was a contestant on the Great British Sewing Bee in 2013.

www.whodunnknit.com
@DeadlyKnitshade
*Lauren O'Farrell*

Lauren is an artist and the founder of the UK's largest craft community, Stitch London.

## ACKNOWLEDGMENTS

**Thanks to Ame Verso, Honor Head, Cath Senker, Jodie Lystor and the whole team at F&W Media for their continued support and amazing patience!**

# NOTES...

Use these pages to jot down references from the book or your own notes...

NOTES...

NOTES...

# INDEX

A DAVID & CHARLES BOOK
© F&W Media International, Ltd 2014

David & Charles is an imprint of F&W Media International, Ltd
Brunel House, Forde Close, Newton Abbot, TQ12 4PU, UK

F&W Media International, Ltd is a subsidiary of F+W Media, Inc
10151 Carver Road, Suite #200, Blue Ash, OH 45242, USA

Images: p2,p3,p4,p5 ©iStock.com/Electric Crayon; p9,p12,p
13,p18,p19,p21,p25,p26,p29,p30,p32,p33,p35,p37 (bottom
left), p40,p42,p43,p44,p45, p49,p51 (top left); p52,p54,p55
(top right), p57,p58,p59,p61,p63,p64 (figure), p67,p71
(figure),p73,p76,p77 (left), p79,p80,p82 (top middle),p83,p84
(bottom left), p86,p87,p88,p89 (top right), p93 (bottom right),
p94,p99,p103 (middle left), p106,p107,p111,p112,p113,p
116,p122,p123 (figure), p125,p126 ©iStock.com/NL shop;
p50,p51(bottom left & top right),p64 (bottom left), p92 (bottom
left), p128 (bottom right) ©iStock.com/Jamtoons; p54 ©iStock.
com/FrankRamspott; p55,p82 (middle right), p89 (bottom
left), p103 (middle right), p119 (bottom right/blue image), p120
(bottom right) ©iStock.com/kimberrywood; p65,p68,p75,p77
(bottom right), p82 (middle left), p84 (bottom right), p85,p91
(top left), p93 (top left) ©iStock.com/saw; p69 (bottom left)
©iStock.com/SamHi; p69 (bottom right) ©iStock.com/
owattaphotos; p91 (bottom left) ©iStock.com/Bulent Ince; p97
(top right) ©iStock.com/ilyast; p119 (top left) ©iStock.com/
YummySuperStar; p123 (bottom left) ©iStock.com/ilyast.
p10,p23,p27,p58 (target), p71 (target), p78,p97 (bottom left),
p119 ( bottom left), p120 (bottom left) ©Shutterstock/NL
Shop; p11,p98 ©Shutterstock/CPDesign; p20 ©Shutterstock/
nopporn; p66 ©Shutterstock/Evgeniy Yatskov; p84( top right),
p92 (bottom left) ©Shutterstock/Bloom Design; p97 (bottom
right) ©Shutterstock/dapoomll; p129 ©Shutterstock/The Last
Word.

First published in the UK and USA in 2014    .

A catalogue record for this book is available from the British
Library.

ISBN-13: 978-1-4463-0489-1 paperback
ISBN-10: 1-4463-0489-2 paperback

ISBN-13: 978-1-4463-6902-9 PDF
ISBN-10: 1-4463-6902-1 PDF

ISBN-13: 978-1-4463-6901-2 EPUB
ISBN-10: 1-4463-6901-3 EPUB

Printed in Slovenia by GPS Group for:
F&W Media International, Ltd
Brunel House, Forde Close, Newton Abbot, TQ12 4PU, UK

10 9 8 7 6 5 4 3 2 1

Acquisitions Editor: Ame Verso
Desk Editor: Honor Head
Project Editor: Cath Senker
Art Editor: Jodie Lystor
Production Manager: Beverley Richardson

F+W Media publishes high quality books on a wide range
of subjects.
For more great book ideas visit: www.stitchcraftcreate.co.uk